MENSA

PUBLICATIONS

WORD GAMES
FOR
KIDS

MENSA

PUBLICATIONS

WORD GAMES

FOR

KIDS

ROBERT ALLEN

P Prima Publishing
3875 Atherton Road
Rocklin, CA 95765
(916) 632 4400

Prima Publishing, Rocklin, CA 95765

Printed and bound in Italy

96 95 94 93 10 9 8 7 6 5 4 3 2 1

Library of Congress Cataloging-in-Publication Data
is available on request

ISBN 1-55958-593-5

★ INTRODUCTION ★

I suppose you're not going to read this, are you? I mean, I don't blame you or anything, I'd probably do the same in your place. If you like messing about with words then by now you'll have plunged into the book and be unscrambling anagrams, crossing crosswords, sorting syllables and generally having fun. The puzzles are divided into six levels of difficulty from easy, Level A, to almost impossible, Level F. Work your way through each level. Even if the higher levels seem really difficult now, once you've done a few they'll seem less daunting.

Of course if you *don't* like words and a well-meaning relative bought this for you because they thought it was educational, then I'm sorry. It's not supposed to be educational. I hope it's engrossing, enchanting, delightful, tantalizing, tormenting and mind-bending. Have a quick look at the puzzles anyway. You never know, you might find out that you *do* like words after all.

If you like puzzles then you would probably like Mensa. It is the only society I know of which lets you in just because you are good at puzzling. We have about 120,000 members throughout the world (with the majority in Great Britain and the U.S.A.). Junior members in British Mensa keep in touch through *Bright Sparks* magazine which appears bi-monthly and contains stories, puzzles, features, a Rage Page (for the seriously enraged), letters, perplexing questions with (we hope) sensible answers, and lots more. The great thing about Mensa is that you get to meet so many people with different interests.

Many thanks to my friend Sarah Picken for all her help in compiling this book.

R. P. Allen

Robert Allen
Editorial Director
Mensa Publications

★ MENSA MINI IQ TEST ★

Take 10 minutes only to complete the test.

1 If a circle is one how many is an octagon?

2 There are 1,200 elephants in a herd. Some have pink and blue stripes, some are all pink and some are all blue. Of these one third are pure pink. Is it true that 400 elephants are definitely blue?

3 Which vowel comes directly between J and T?

4 Which number comes next in this series of numbers?

1 2 3 5 7 11 13 ?

5 Which letter comes next in this series of letters?

B A C B D C E D F ?

6 Which of these is the odd one out?

CAT DOG HAMSTER
RABBIT ELK

7 Which word can be added to the end of GRASS and the beginning of SCAPE to form two other English words?

8 The zoo has two lions. A lion eats three pounds of meat each day. A lioness eats two pounds of meat each day and a lion cub eats one pound of meat. The delivery for today is two pounds of meat and that is all the meat available for the zoo. Must any or both of the lions go hungry?

9 If six minus one is worth nine and seven minus five is worth one. How much is six plus ten worth?

10 Which word of four letters can be added to the front of the following words to create other English words?

CARD BOX BAG HASTE

ANSWERS

1 8.
2 No.
3 O.
4 17. (They are all prime numbers.)
5 E.
6 Elk.
7 Land.
8 No, they could be lion cubs.
9 9. Value of Roman numerals in words, if any, either subtracted or added.
10 Post.

Score	Comment	Possible IQ
10	Excellent	160
9	Very Good Indeed	155
8	Mensa Level	148
7	Good	130
6	Above Average	115
5	Average	100
4	Below Average	90
3	Well Below Average	80
2	Poor	65
1	Very Poor Indeed	50

NOW TRY THIS ONE:
Your watch was correct at midnight but then began to gain two and a half minutes every hour. It stopped two hours ago showing quarter past six in the morning. What should the watch be showing?

If you think you have the correct answer send it to Mensa on a postcard or the back of an envelope and you will receive a certificate of merit, along with Mensa details. The address to reply to is:
MENSA HOUSE, ST JOHN'S SQUARE, WOLVERHAMPTON WV2 1AH, ENGLAND.

THUMB SUCKERS

★ LEVEL A ★

PUZZLE 1

Below you'll find a pyramid. Using the clues, fill in the correct words. To help you, to make the new word a letter is added to the end of the previous word each time.

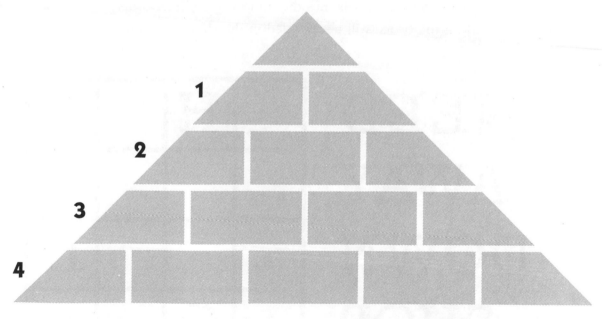

1. A term of endearment for your father.

2. You can cook dinner in this.

3 Found in a window.

4. A group of entertainers appearing as contestants in a TV quiz show.

ANSWER NO.54

PUZZLE 2

The sentence below is a well known quotation.
We have used a simple trick to obscure the meaning. Can you unscramble it?

WTOB ABEL FORC GNOTH ATOS OBER, ATHATI HIST ATHEM BQUESTIONA.

◆?◆ ANSWER NO.63 ◆?◆

PUZZLE 3

If you fill the four words into the grid in the correct order,
something found on the beach will be revealed in the shaded column. What is it?

NEED
AWAY
DOWN
SHOP

◆?◆ ANSWER NO.81 ◆?◆

PUZZLE 4

When animals are grouped together we have some very interesting names to describe the groups, for example a murder of crows. Here are some easy ones to get you started.

A - - - - - of cows.
A - - - - - - - of hens.
A - - - - - - - of geese.
A - - - - - - of lions.
A - - - - - - - of fish.

?⟩ANSWER NO.116⟨?

PUZZLE 5

Below you will find a number of characters from books and rhymes whose names have been mixed up. Can you put them together again and find the odd one out?

CAPTAIN

CHRISTOPHER

PETER

MOTHER

PAN

BETTY

ROBIN

HUMPTY

HOOK

GOOSE

BOTTER

DUMPTY

LUCY

?⟩ANSWER NO.18⟨?

PUZZLE 6

The faces below have been made up out of letters.
If you unravel them you will find the names of the people.

? ANSWER NO.99 ?

PUZZLE 7

What kind of a father goes round dressed all in red, and never cuts his beard,
and works only one day a year? Unjumble the letters and you will find out

FATHER HSARSMITC

? ANSWER NO.36 ?

PUZZLE 8

One of these tins of paint does not
go with the others, which is it?

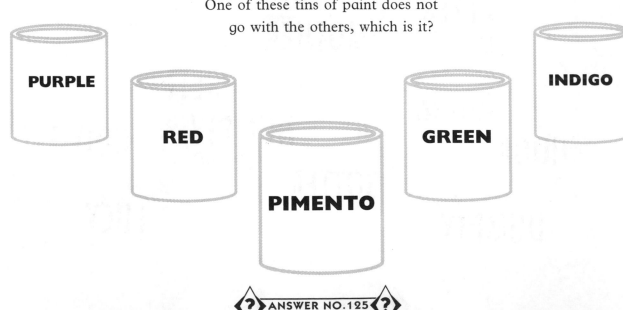

PURPLE

RED

PIMENTO

GREEN

INDIGO

? ANSWER NO.125 ?

PUZZLE 9

The clues below will help you to find words to fill the spaces.
To help you even more we can tell you that the first syllable of each word
could be found in a paint box.

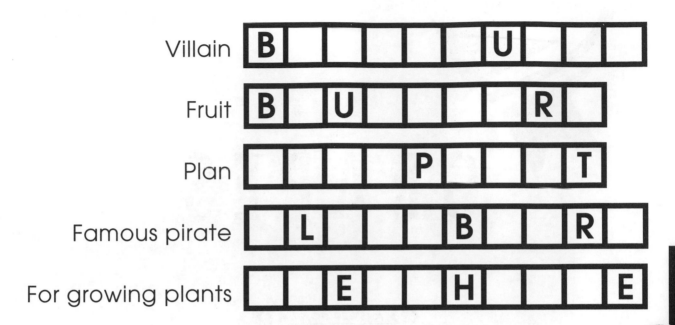

Villain | B | | | | | U | | |

Fruit | B | U | | | | R |

Plan | | | | P | | | T |

Famous pirate | | L | | | B | | R | |

For growing plants | | | E | | | H | | | E |

ANSWER NO.142

PUZZLE 10

Below you'll find anagrams of four common pets. Which ones?

1. **tca**

2. **dgo**

3. **hifs**

4. **sahmter**

ANSWER NO.167

LEVEL A

PUZZLE 11

Who ate the grapes? Look at the word and see if you can find a four-letter word describing the culprits.

 ANSWER NO.27

PUZZLE 12

The bear had a sore head. He was not in a good mood.
In fact he was in a really awful mood. Take the jumbled letters below and add them to the word bear to make one word which will show you just how bad he was feeling.

E   B   N

L   A   U

- -   - -   B E A R - - -   - - -

 ANSWER NO.45

PUZZLE 13

Fill in the words in the correct order and in the shaded column
you will be able to see something that comes out at night.

FORK
KNEE
POLE
OMEN

ANSWER NO.80

PUZZLE 14

If you solve these anagrams you will reveal four numbers.
What is the total of all the numbers added together?

1. **ofur**

2. **vesen**

3. **noe**

4. **ixs**

ANSWER NO.98

LEVEL A

PUZZLE 15

Look at the words on the chalk board, which is the odd one out?

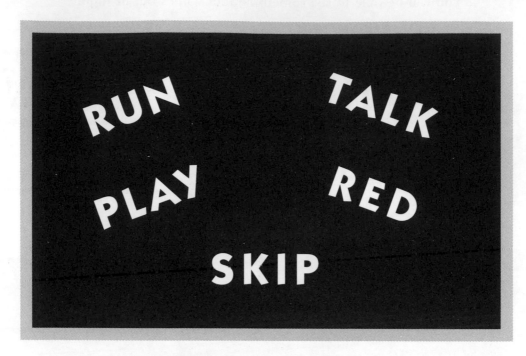

ANSWER NO.9

PUZZLE 16

When rearranged, the anagrams below will turn into four types of weather.
Can you work out what they are?

1. **arin**

2. **usn**

3. **nsow**

4. **ahil**

ANSWER NO.124

PUZZLE 17

Mrs Jones was very proud of her garden. She had the best asters in the county.
That is until next door's dog decided to bury his bone under them.
Add the three jumbled up letters to the front of the word aster
and make a new word telling you what happened.

— — — ASTER

?⟩ ANSWER NO.141 ⟨?

PUZZLE 18

The faces below have been made up out of letters.
If you unravel them you will find the names of the people.

?⟩ ANSWER NO.168 ⟨?

LEVEL A

The birds were just enjoying a few well-earned crumbs in the garden when along came that mean and murderous cat from the house round the corner. What did the birds do? Add the jumbled letters to the word cat and you will get the answer.

R S
E T

– C A T – – – –

? ANSWER NO.64 ?

PUZZLE 20

If you fill in these four words correctly you will find a
type of flower in the shaded column.

BOOK
CHEF
VASE
BIRD

? ANSWER NO.151 ?

PUZZLE 21

At the zoo the monkeys were throwing oranges at each other.
If you look closely at the word orange you will see a three-letter word
which tells you what the keeper did.

? ANSWER NO.53 ?

PUZZLE 22

The planets in the night sky have an intruder
among them. Which is it?

EARTH

MARS

VERMICELLI

SATURN

MERCURY

? ANSWER NO.62 ?

Can you find the word ELEMENT? It appears only once
in a horizontal, vertical or diagonal line.

E	L	M	E	N	T	E	L	E	M
L	E	E	L	E	N	M	E	N	T
M	E	N	T	E	L	M	E	N	T
E	L	E	M	E	N	E	L	M	E
E	M	E	N	T	E	L	E	M	E
L	M	E	L	E	M	E	M	T	N
E	E	L	M	E	N	T	E	L	E
M	N	T	E	L	E	M	N	E	T
E	T	E	M	E	N	E	T	L	E
N	E	L	E	M	E	N	E	N	T

THUMB SUCKERS

◈ ? ◈ ANSWER NO.82 ◈ ? ◈

PUZZLE 24

It's bedtime but are you sleepy? No! Now what should we try?
Unravel the letters below and you will come up with a suggestion.

BEDTIME ROTSY

◈ ? ◈ ANSWER NO.115 ◈ ? ◈

PUZZLE 25

Can you solve these anagrams to reveal four well-known parts of the body?

1. ram

2. ahed

3. elg

4. ofot

 ANSWER NO.17

PUZZLE 26

Have you had enough of school? Well, just unravel the jumbled letters and add them to the word play. Then relax.

PLAY EMIT

 ANSWER NO.100

PUZZLE 27

This is one strange dog! If you take the two groups of mixed-up letters and add one to the front and one to the end you will come up with the seven-letter names of two very different creatures.

L U L L B H I S S F

DOG

LEVEL A

 ANSWER NO.35

PUZZLE 28

Place the words into the grid in such a way that something hot can be seen in the shaded column.

ACHE

WOLF

HAIR

TAXI

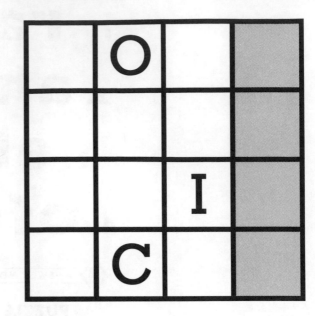

? ANSWER NO.126 ?

PUZZLE 29

Look carefully at the caterpillar. See if you can find a three-letter word which tells you what happened to the apple. Caterpillars should only eat leaves, so he felt sick. See if you can also find a four-letter word which tells what he took to feel better.

CATERPILLAR

? ANSWER NO.143 ?

PUZZLE 30

Teddy isn't a boy and he isn't a dog, he isn't a tomato and he isn't a frog.
If you unravel the letters with care you will discover that he is a...

TEDDY AREB

 ANSWER NO.166

PUZZLE 31

Take a look at the names on the children's school bags. Which is the odd one out?

ANSWER NO.26

PUZZLE 32

It was the highlight of the display. A giant firework! But what sort was it going to be? Just unscramble the letters below to find the answer.

CATHERINE LEWEH

ANSWER NO.44

PUZZLE 33

Milo got into old Mr Jimson's orchard and guzzled his peaches happily all afternoon. But that night the fruit had its revenge! Take a look at the word peaches and try to find a five-letter word which describes just how Milo's tummy felt.

PEACHES

ANSWER NO.79

PUZZLE 34

Now we're really going to rock you! But how? With a track from the latest album by Total Cosmic Disaster? Aren't you just a little young for that kind of music? Why not just rearrange the jumbled letters below and come up with a swinging solution.

ROCKING SRHOE

ANSWER NO.97

PENCIL CHEWERS

★ LEVEL B ★

PUZZLE 35

Look at the farm gate. It may look like alphabet soup to you but, if you start with
the first H and then take every fifth letter, you will be able to find an animal who lives on
the farm. Try again starting with the G, then the M and so on.

There are five hidden animals.

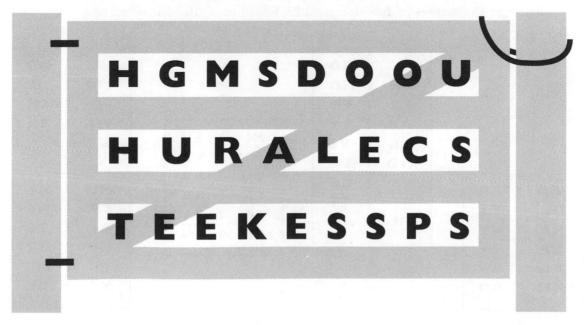

HGMSDOOU

HURALECS

TEEKESSPS

‹?› ANSWER NO.8 ‹?›

PUZZLE 36

Walter Foole has taken a job at the local library. Oh well, once a Foole always a Foole and he has already accidentally removed the name labels from several shelves. Try to sort them all out before the librarian finds out and marks Walter's card.

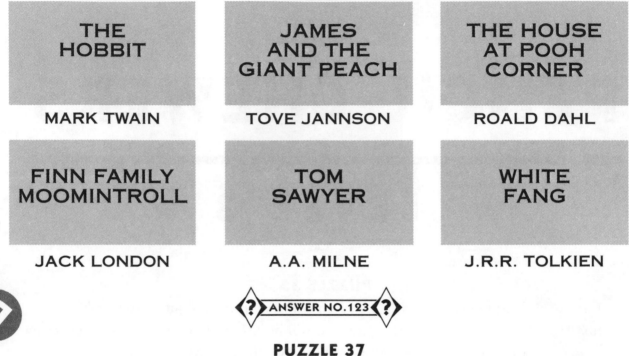

THE HOBBIT	JAMES AND THE GIANT PEACH	THE HOUSE AT POOH CORNER
MARK TWAIN	TOVE JANNSON	ROALD DAHL
FINN FAMILY MOOMINTROLL	TOM SAWYER	WHITE FANG
JACK LONDON	A.A. MILNE	J.R.R. TOLKIEN

◆?► ANSWER NO. 123 ◄?◆

PUZZLE 37

Replace each question mark with a letter to form a word. Reading down you should discover the names of five things to be found in a kitchen. What are they?

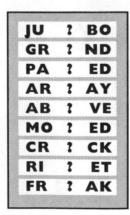

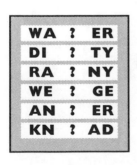

```
JU ? BO
GR ? ND
PA ? ED
AR ? AY
AB ? VE
MO ? ED
CR ? CK
RI ? ET
FR ? AK
```

```
HI ? ER
AM ? ND
OU ? ER
EX ? RA
SA ? TY
ST ? RN
```

```
BL ? OD
MO ? IE
FR ? SH
MA ? IA
```

```
WA ? ER
DI ? TY
RA ? NY
WE ? GE
AN ? ER
KN ? AD
```

```
HU ? KY
CR ? NE
AC ? TE
IN ? UR
TH ? ME
VE ? GE
```

◆?► ANSWER NO. 140 ◄?◆

PUZZLE 38

All the well-known sayings have a word missing.
Complete them by taking words from the group on the right.

1. Too many chiefs and not enough ?

2. Many hands make ? work

3. An ? a day keeps the
   doctor away

4. A new broom ? clean

5. A stitch in time saves ?

6. Cut your coat according
   to your ?

7. When the ? away the
   mice will play

8. Can't see the wood for the ?

9. All's well that ends?

10. It's an ill ? that blows nobody any good

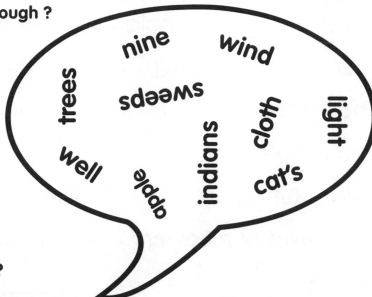

 ANSWER NO.169

PUZZLE 39

The letters on the computer screen make a series.
Work out the logic and replace the question mark.

ANSWER NO.65

PUZZLE 40

The answers to the six clues below are all anagrams of each other. What are they?

Small piece of wire driven through
sheets of paper to hold them together....

A crayon for drawing ....

The lightest hue ....

You eat off them ....

Folds often found in a girl's skirt ....

The leaves of a flower..............................

ANSWER NO.152

B

PUZZLE 41

Each of the following sets of clues should give you a pair of homophones
(words that sound the same but have different meanings).

NAKED		CARNIVORE
RODENT		BODY COVERING
DEER		BLOOD PUMP
BAMBI		BELOVED
PLANT		RECOGNISE WRITING
SUGAR PLANT		DEFEAT

ANSWER NO.52

PUZZLE 42

The diagram shows a plan of the secret headquarters of the dreaded Crime Syndicate International. By following the instructions clearly you can reach the Boss's office and apprehend him. Exciting, isn't it?

Start at the square two places south of the one in the middle of the top line. Go 1 square east and 2 south. Now go 2 squares west and 4 north. The room you want is now 1 square SE.

Which is the final square?

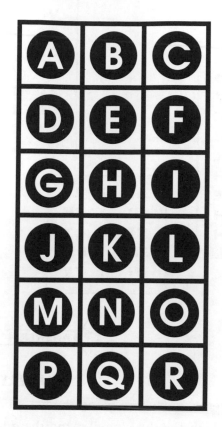

 ANSWER NO.61

PUZZLE 43

The following sentence has two gaps which can be filled with words using the same seven letters.

The _ _ _ _ _ _ _ felt lonely on the frontier and longed for _ _ _ _ _ _ _ from home.

 ANSWER NO.83

PUZZLE 44

Replace each question mark with a letter to form a word. Reading down you should discover the names of five jobs. What are they?

VI	?	AL
GR	?	ET
DR	?	WN
UL	?	ER
ET	?	IC
GL	?	AM
HO	?	SE

ER	?	SE
MI	?	RO
FA	?	ET
CH	?	RE
RO	?	TE
FI	?	AL
WA	?	CH
GR	?	DE
PI	?	CH
WI	?	CH

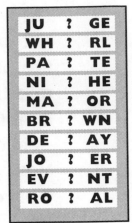

JU	?	GE
WH	?	RL
PA	?	TE
NI	?	HE
MA	?	OR
BR	?	WN
DE	?	AY
JO	?	ER
EV	?	NT
RO	?	AL

AM	?	LE
FR	?	SK
HO	?	LY
SH	?	RN
WI	?	TY

PI	?	CH
ER	?	PT
FA	?	CE
AI	?	LE
CH	?	AP

 ANSWER NO.114

PUZZLE 45

Add a letter anywhere along the length of each word to make another word which fits the clue. Taking the added letters in order, the name of a girl will be revealed. Which one?

☐ 1. SELL — an odour
☐ 2. MAD — a female servant
☐ 3. HEAP — not expensive
☐ 4. TANK — to show your gratitude
☐ 5. PACE — opposite of war
☐ 6. FOG — to beat severely
☐ 7. WED — to fuse bits of metal together by heating
☐ 8. BARD — hair found on the face

 ANSWER NO.16

PUZZLE 46

The creepie crawlies pictured have their names listed in code.
Just to make the game more interesting we have mixed them all up.
Leaving out "J", create a 5 x 5 grid with the letters A–E being A1 to A5,
F–K B1 to B5, etc. Use these codes to solve the puzzle.

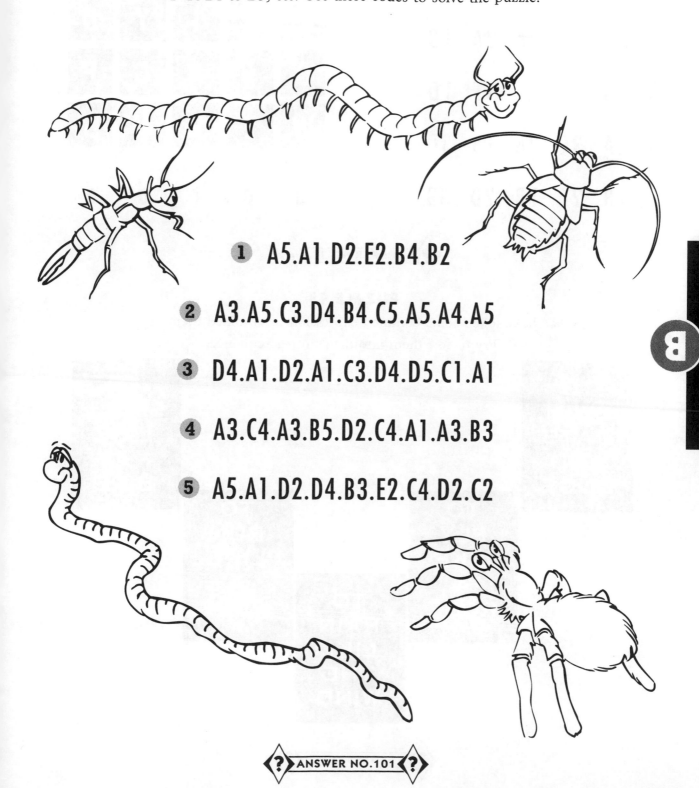

1 A5.A1.D2.E2.B4.B2

2 A3.A5.C3.D4.B4.C5.A5.A4.A5

3 D4.A1.D2.A1.C3.D4.D5.C1.A1

4 A3.C4.A3.B5.D2.C4.A1.A3.B3

5 A5.A1.D2.D4.B3.E2.C4.D2.C2

LEVEL B

B

ANSWER NO.101

PUZZLE 47

Can you work out the five words below?

1. 3D 3B 1C 2D 3C

2. 3E 3D 2A 3A 1D

3. 1B 3B 2C 1E 1D

4. 1A 3C 2A 1B 3D

5. 2B 2C 1B 2D 3B

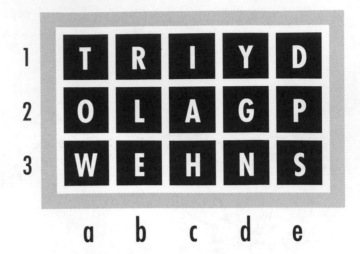

	a	b	c	d	e
1	T	R	I	Y	D
2	O	L	A	G	P
3	W	E	H	N	S

ANSWER NO.34

PUZZLE 48

We have taken some common expressions and mixed them up.
Try to sort them into their proper sequence.

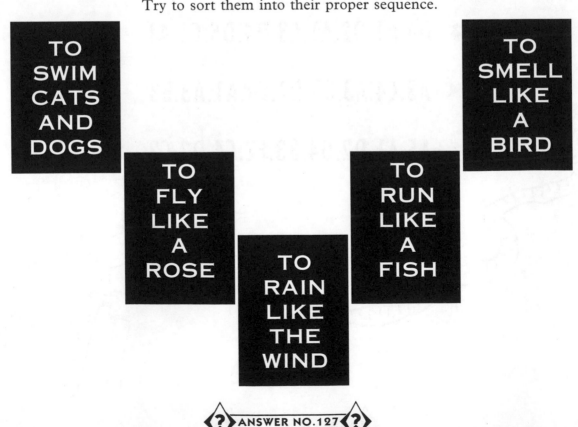

TO SWIM CATS AND DOGS

TO SMELL LIKE A BIRD

TO FLY LIKE A ROSE

TO RUN LIKE A FISH

TO RAIN LIKE THE WIND

ANSWER NO.127

PUZZLE 49

The following are nicknames which have been mixed up.
Some of them belong to things and some to people. When you have
sorted them out you should find one pair which doesn't fit.

BIG

OLD

UNION

BLUE

GREEN

STORMIN'

BRIAN

BEARD

NORMAN

GLORY

BEN

JACK

?ANSWER NO.144?

PUZZLE 50

Find the letter to place at the centre of the wheel which will turn
all the spokes into five-letter words. Each word starts with the same letter.

?ANSWER NO.165?

PUZZLE 51

In a twisted, mind-bending sort of way the following words form a series.
Which is the odd one out?

Adverb
Card
Engulf
Become
Grouch

◆? ANSWER NO.25 ?◆

PUZZLE 52

In Madame Twoswords' famous waxworks Walter Foole,
the newest assistant, has mixed up the labels on the dummies.
Can you sort them out and help this dummy keep his job?

OLIVER	WASHINGTON
MAHATMA	ROBERTS
MICHELLE	CROMWELL
GEORGE	GANDHI
ROBIN	PFEIFFER
JULIA	CODY
WILLIAM	HOOD

◆? ANSWER NO.43 ?◆

PUZZLE 53

Add one letter to each line which will end the left word and start the right word, changing both into new English words. Reading down, a popular star from the world of sport will be revealed. Which one?

SAG	?	WASH
THROW	?	ARROW
FIRE	?	ARK
PRIME	?	ANGER
HER	?	LOPE
DRAM	?	VERSION
BE	?	RATE
ARE	?	BATE
FORGE	?	CUBA
PEN	?	LEDGE
YET	?	RATE

ANSWER NO.78

LEVEL B

PUZZLE 54

The answers to the five clues below are all anagrams of one another.
What are the words?

Something left over.............................

Fruits that grow on trees........................

He clears the field of a crop....................

She cuts off the outer surface................

Ancient battle weapon ....

ANSWER NO.96

PUZZLE 55

It is now Walter's second day working at the world renowned waxworks of Madame Twoswords and he's gone and mixed up the first names and surnames of the models. Having sorted the labels into equal piles, can you help put them in the right order before Madame has poor Walter coated in wax and put on display.

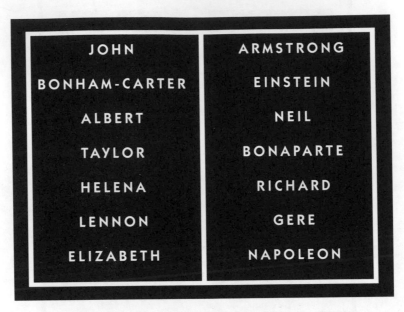

JOHN	ARMSTRONG
BONHAM-CARTER	EINSTEIN
ALBERT	NEIL
TAYLOR	BONAPARTE
HELENA	RICHARD
LENNON	GERE
ELIZABETH	NAPOLEON

ANSWER NO. 7

PUZZLE 56

The answers to these ten clues all rhyme. What are they?

1. Reptile or unpleasant person. ☐
2. A dull persistent pain. ☐
3. One way to cook potatoes. ☐
4. An implement used in the garden. ☐
5. To rouse from sleep ☐
6. To abandon someone. ☐
7. A large body of water. ☐
8. To fracture an arm. ☐
9. Marker in the ground. ☐
10. To falsify. ☐

ANSWER NO. 122

PUZZLE 57

The answers to the five clues below all rhyme.
What are they?

1. Unswerving in allegiance.
2. To ruin.
3. Their blood might be blue.
4. Hard work.
5. Grotesque spout on roof.

 ANSWER NO.139

PUZZLE 58

You are hunting the autograph of Mucho Macho the film star.
You know the right street but not the number.
Here are some clues to help you find the house.

1. Mucho is much too macho to have flowers in his garden.

2. The number of the house cannot be divided by 7.

3. The house is not called Sunshine Cottage.

4. If the house number is divided by two the result is between 15 and 17.

5. Mucho made a film called 'Moon Mission'. It bombed.

6. Mucho is a known cat lover.

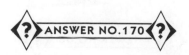 ANSWER NO.170

LEVEL B

NAIL NIBBLERS

★ LEVEL C ★

PUZZLE 59

The following strings of letters are all anagrams of well known cities. But each one contains an extra letter. Throw all the extra letters in the bin and you will have the name of one of the States of America.

dilnono

rapids

amore

shallad

oookyt

ANSWER NO.66

PUZZLE 60

Remove ten letters to leave a dead language.

C A L S B A R E T T I P N O R

? ANSWER NO.153 **?**

PUZZLE 61

The letters below spell out six three-letter words. The letters of each word are in different type styles but always in the same order. The order is this

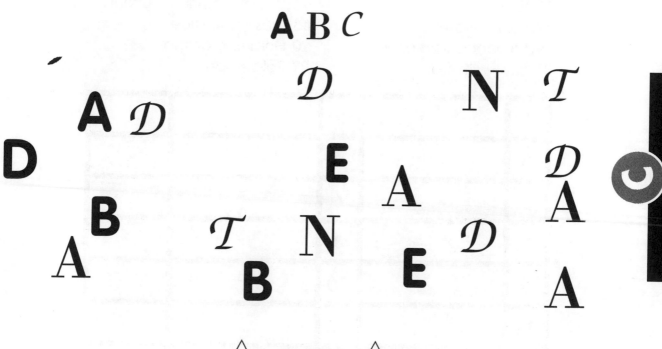

? ANSWER NO.51 **?**

PUZZLE 62

The following groups of letters are all names of countries from which two-letter 'heads' and 'tails' have been removed. How many can you recognise?

RTUG   NGA   MAN   RMA   EE

? ANSWER NO.60 **?**

LEVEL C

PUZZLE 63

Solve the clues and write the answers in the appropriate boxes.
The right-hand answer will always be the same as the left-hand answer, except that one letter will be missing. Write the missing letter in the box on the far right, and reading down you will discover the name of a sauce.

1. DIsplay
3. Shop available for business
5. Not the back
7. Mad
9. Awareness of danger
11. A fish
13. Tidy
15. Wet
17. Falling water
19. Someone who annoys
21. Blow with axe

2. Pig
4. What you write with
6. Place for baptism
8. Silly
10. A long way
12. Hat
14. Device for catching fish
16. Unit of electrical current
18. Was in the race
20. Domestic animal
22. Policeman

1		2		
3		4		
5		6		
7		8		
9		10		
11		12		
13		14		
15		16		
17		18		
19		20		
21		22		

 ANSWER NO.84

PUZZLE 64

Find a four-letter word which can be added to the end of the words of the left-hand column and the beginning of the words in the right-hand column to give 10 new words.

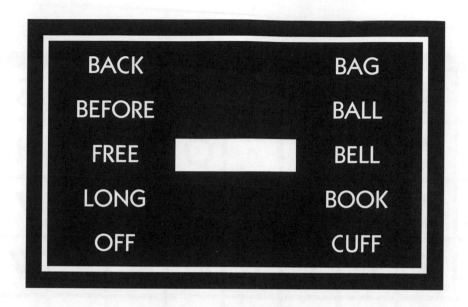

BACK		BAG
BEFORE		BALL
FREE		BELL
LONG		BOOK
OFF		CUFF

ANSWER NO.113

PUZZLE 65

Re-arrange the letters in the grid to find the name of a computer game hero.

S	C	E	E
T	N	H	O
D	I	H	G
O	H	E	G

ANSWER NO.15

LEVEL C

PUZZLE 66

Identify the animals and fish concealed among the letters.
The words may run in any direction and may overlap.

T	A	B	E	A	R	G	S	G	A
P	C	O	D	F	O	T	S	H	B
A	G	O	T	R	Q	U	N	V	D
R	T	H	F	L	M	N	A	W	R
R	C	I	D	E	S	A	K	K	A
O	R	S	G	T	U	N	E	L	P
T	A	V	T	E	C	B	O	P	O
U	G	Z	Q	S	R	L	J	R	E
H	I	Y	E	K	N	O	M	E	L
C	E	L	E	P	H	A	N	T	D

ANSWER NO.102

PUZZLE 67

Find a word or name that goes with the one we have given and then read down the first letter of each answer. You should find a nameless word!

	pie
	conquest
	singer
	watchman
	fever
	Twain
	poppy
	duckling
	spray

? ANSWER NO.33 ?

PUZZLE 68

The letters written on the petals contain anagrams of five common wild flowers. Can you name them?

? ANSWER NO.128 ?

LEVEL C

PUZZLE 69

Below you'll find a list of words containing 'E' as their only vowel.
Can you locate them in the big 'E' shape? Which is the word that appears twice?

BEETLE   EFFECT   HERE   MESSENGER   PEPPER   TEPEE

CEMETERY   ENTENTE   JESTER   MERGE   REFEREE   VESSEL

CLEVER   FERMENT   KESTREL   METHYLENE   REFERENCE   WHEREVER

CRESCENT   GREENERY   LETTER   NEEDLE   SEETHE   YEN

DETERGENT   HELMET   MEDLEY   NETTLES   THEME

```
M Y R E F E R E N C E N R Y R R K E
E E N V E S E R E V E R E H W W E S
S N E C E F F E C T Y M T E S S S E
Y T E E G E R F L S E E T E N N R S
R S D N R K E R E H S F E D B B N P
E E L S E R J E T E F E L T H H Y E
N J E S M R E
E H T E E S Y
E E N T J E T B Y F L E C H T E K R
R T P N Y E E R F E S E L T T E N E
G R E E T P M T E P L G E N E R E P
F R E G N E S S E M R D V E V C F P
E V T R E T L E T E M L E E H R F E
E E N E C P R R E M S E R L M Y R P
L Y K T S P E
C R R E E K H
V E E D R E C E B E V G Y F E E R I
E T T F C S E E N E L Y H T E M H E
T E S S E T F L S M E T S E C S E M
E M E E F R F S T E S T E M L E H E
N E J R B E E T R E F E L X J V E H
T C E C R L M E T N E T N E E N E T
```

ANSWER NO.145

PUZZLE 70

Solve the clues and you will find that the first letter of the answers make a word when read down. Clue: May be shocking.

Clue	Answer
Natural force	
Greater in length	
Live coal	
British sport	
Medicine in pill form	
Herb with girl's name	
Herb found in pizza	
Walk slowly	
Never-ending	

? ANSWER NO.164 ?

PUZZLE 71

When you solve these clues and fill the answers into the grid you will find that it reads the same down and across.

1. **Not slow.**

2. **A particular piece of ground.**

3. **In a tennis match there are a maximum of five.**

4. **A piece of work to be done.**

? ANSWER NO.24 ?

PUZZLE 72

The new postman has been given an important parcel to deliver to the
house of Pearl Precious, the movie star. He doesn't know the exact
number of the house but the guys at the sorting office have given him a few clues.
See if you can help him to find the right house

**1. Pearl Precious has
no pets.**

**2. The number of her
house cannot be
divided by 3.**

**3. Pearl does not have
milk delivered.**

4. Pearl hates flowers.

**5. The number of the
house is not a prime
number.**

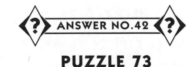 ANSWER NO.42

PUZZLE 73

Put a word in the middle space which makes, when added to the end of the words on the
left and the beginning of the words on the right, eight new eight-letter words.

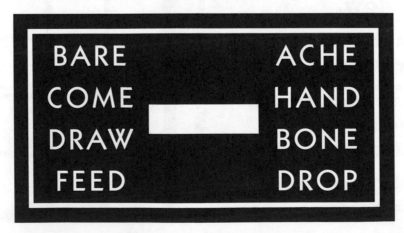

BARE   ACHE
COME   HAND
DRAW   BONE
FEED   DROP

 ANSWER NO.77

PUZZLE 74

Take a letter from each cloud in turn and make four words connected with bad weather.

ANSWER NO.95

PUZZLE 75

When you have solved all the clues, read the first letter of the answers
and you will find a hidden word. The clue is a mystery.

Clue	Answer
Violet	
Quantity	
Agreement	
Athletic competition	
Sub-continent	
Adhesive	
Wet weather gear	
Pachyderm	

? ANSWER NO.6 **?**

PUZZLE 76

The diagram shows the front of a very clever type of safe.
Turn each wheel in the order given and you will be able to open the door.
What is the proper order?

The final square is to the south of the square two places east of the square which is one place due south of the square at the extreme north west.

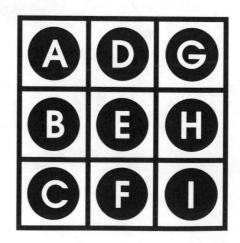

```
N
W ↑ E
  S
```

? ANSWER NO.121 **?**

PUZZLE 77

Eight kids are hiding in the grid below hoping to avoid school.
Their names are: PETE, SUSIE, DICK, MICHELLE, JOSII,
HOLLY, LARRY, and JULIA. Can you find them?
The names may be spelt in any direction, not necessarily in a straight line..

J	H	A	C	D	J	U	L	V	Q
O	S	R	T	S	U	L	N	I	P
A	P	V	D	N	E	S	I	E	A
N	E	W	K	I	P	Q	U	R	H
C	T	E	L	J	C	S	O	G	T
Y	Q	T	E	I	U	K	Z	X	C
R	E	L	L	E	H	C	I	M	R
R	V	A	K	L	T	E	B	O	J
A	T	U	H	O	L	L	Y	Y	S
L	K	L	H	O	P	R	U	T	G

LEVEL C

PUZZLE 78

The following sentences have been written in a special way to hide their meaning.
If you look at them carefully you may get the message.

RGELA HANTSELEP DOMSEL KLWA CKLYQUI

TERSHAMS ERNEV KETA NCHLU THWI DILESCROCO

ENEV LLSMA FFESGIRA EPSLE DINGSTAN

IFULBEAUT RFLIESBUTTE TERFLIT ONGAM WERSFLO

ANTGI DASPAN ELLDW ONGAM BOOBAM VESGRO

 ANSWER NO.171

PUZZLE 79

The following are books in which the words have been jumbled.
Can you sort them out?

THE OF MOHICANS LAST THE

PRAIRIE THE HOUSE LITTLE THE ON

CENTRE THE TO EARTH OF JOURNEY TO

THOUSAND SEA UNDER LEAGUES TWENTY THE

SERVICE HER SECRET MAJESTY'S ON

 ANSWER NO.67

PUZZLE 80

When you have solved the clues you will find that the first letter of the answers will give a hidden word reading down.

Instrument for giving commands	
Assault	
Fighting vehicle	
Strategy	
Not yet a captain	
Foe	

Clue: Part of a war

ANSWER NO.154

PUZZLE 81

The jumbled words in the bubbles are all languages.
How many can you unscramble?

ANSWER NO.50

LEVEL C

PUZZLE 82

The letters on the side of the glue pot make the word adhesives.
How many words of four letters or more can you make out of the nine letters given?

ANSWER NO.59

PUZZLE 83

The answer to each line becomes part of the clue to the next one.
What are the seven words?

The first word is good to spend;

Change the first letter for something to eat;

Add a letter in front for a sham;

Drop the last letter to have a long-distance chat;

Drop the first letter, change the third for where you live;

Change the third but don't fall in this;

Change the first letter to leave you with a burrowing animal.

 ANSWER NO.85

PUZZLE 84

The words below have had letters replaced by playing card symbols.
Each symbol always stands for the same letter. Can you work out
what the words should be? We have given some clues to help.

BU♥♥♠♦ — yellow spread

♥O♥♥♠♦ — unsteady walk

BA♦♦♠♣ — contains water?

♣ONG♠♦ — increased length

♦UBB♣♠ — broken stones

♥O♥A♣S — sums

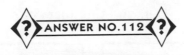 ANSWER NO.112

PUZZLE 85

This fairy tale character became confused after failing to recognise her grandmother.
Can you sort her out?

EIGHT TENDRIL IDOL ROD

 ANSWER NO.14

PUZZLE 86

The sentences below conceal the names of countries.
All the letters are in the right order.

The names are well hidden, mark my words!
I can adamantly state you will not find them.
It will anger many of you to search in vain.
But do not let your ire land you in trouble.
Attack the problem with new zeal and
overcome it.

ANSWER NO.103

PUZZLE 87

Each of the groups of words below has an odd one out.
Can you find them all?

CHEESE MILK BUTTER EGGS	JANUARY SEPTEMBER AUGUST DECEMBER	SPIDER ANT CRICKET BUTTERFLY	ENGLAND SPAIN GREECE POLAND
CALIFORNIA UTAH TEXAS NOVA SCOTIA	JAGUAR LINCOLN HARLEY- DAVIDSON PORSCHE	GANGES THAMES MISSISSIPPI CAMBRIDGE	CUMULUS NIMBUS CYCLONE STRATUS

ANSWER NO.32

PUZZLE 88

Below are ten clues. To help you solve them,
we've supplied the vowels for each answer.

1. To turn about on a axis   `[ ][O][ ][A][ ][E]`

2. Juicy   `[ ][U][ ][U][E][ ]`

3. Helps after dinner   `[ ][I][ ][ ][A][ ][E][ ]`

4. Unfriendly   `[ ][O][ ][I][E]`

5. Of the night   `[ ][O][ ][U][ ][A][ ]`

6. A border between two countries   `[ ][ ][O][ ][I][E][ ]`

7. To tear roughly   `[ ][A][E][A][E]`

8. To unroll a flag   `[U][ ][U][ ][ ]`

9. To have an unjust opinion of   `[ ][I][ ][U][ ][E]`

10. Four times a year   `[ ][U][A][ ][E][ ][ ]`

ANSWER NO.129

LEVEL C

PUZZLE 89

The answer to each line becomes part of the clue to the next one.
What are the seven words?

The first word has already been said;

Remove the third letter for a clenched hand;

Jumble the letters to put through a sieve;

Change the first to raise weights in sport and body building;

Jumble the letters to fly from here to there;

Remove the second to be in good shape;

Change the last for an edible fruit.

ANSWER NO.146

PUZZLE 90

Below you'll find a list of rock and pop stars. All of them, except one, can be found hidden in the word search. Which one is missing? The names you have to find may be written forwards, backwards, upwards, downwards or diagonally.

Alexander O'Neal
Amy Grant
Belinda Carlisle
Billy Joel
Bobby Brown
Bon Jovi
Bruce Springsteen
Cathy Dennis
Cher

Debbie Gibson
En Vogue
Heart
Jade
Janet Jackson
Madonna
Mariah Carey
Martika
Michael Jackson

New Kids on the Block
Prince
REM
Richard Marx
Right Said Fred
Take That
Whitney Houston
Wilson Philips

ANSWER NO.163

PUZZLE 91

The words of these famous proverbs have been jumbled up.
Can you unravel them?

1 Lady never won fair faint heart.

2 The bush is worth in the two hand in a bird.

3 No spilt crying it's milk use over.

4 Glass shouldn't live in stones houses who throw people.

 ANSWER NO.23

PUZZLE 92

Try to find out the name of this fairy tale character.
Come to think of it, that was the point of the story!

SLIP MILK ENTRUSTS

 ANSWER NO.41

LEVEL C

PUZZLE 93

These film titles are written without vowels.
Your task is to find the missing vowels and reveal the film.

1. TH WZRD F Z
2. CLS NCNTRS F TH THRD KND
3. PLLYNN
4. BCK T TH FTR
5. NTNL VLVT
6. BTMN RTRNS
7. BTY ND TH BST
8. HNY SHRNK TH KDS
9. TH SND F MSC
10. JRSSC PRK

? ANSWER NO.176 ?

PUZZLE 94

By moving one square up, down, right or left – not diagonally – follow the
trail of letters in the grid and you will find the title of a Steven Spielberg film.
But beware, there are six dummy letters included.

T	A	R	K	A
S	E	A	A	R
O	F	O	I	D
L	T	S	R	E
E	H	S	E	R

? ANSWER NO.94 ?

PUZZLE 95

This kid stayed out late and lost her footing. Can you unscramble her and give the tale a happy ending?

ANSWER NO.5

PUZZLE 96

The words below spell out four well-known phrases. The first word of each line is in the right place but the others have been mixed up so that, although the word is in the right place within a line, it has been moved up or down and is now in the wrong line. You have to sort them out. To help you there is a clue for each line.

Here	big	the	she	and	grand	bush
What	lion	eyes	you	lost	her	wardrobe
The	Bo	go	witch	have	mulberry	sheep
Little	we	Peep	round	the	the	mama

Clues: Line 1. Nursery Rhyme
Line 2. Little Red Riding Hood
Line 3. Narnia
Line 4. Careless Shepherdess

ANSWER NO.120

LEVEL C

PUZZLE 97

Can you decipher these film titles?

1 Excellent and Adventure Ted's Bill.

2 Eighty in Around Days World the.

3 of Purple Cairo The Rose.

4 an Stepmother My Alien is.

5 Being Importance The Earnest of.

 ANSWER NO.137

PUZZLE 98

The following proverbs have been rewritten using a long word or words where a short one would have been better! See if you can work out what we mean.

1. It is a malicious shift of atmospheric pressure which fails to produce benefits for some members of the population.

2. A surfeit of hard labour unmixed with recreational activities has the unfortunate effect of making Jack a rather uninteresting youth.

3. An excessive number of culinary operatives tends to have an extremely adverse effect upon the quality of the pottage.

4. It is said to be impossible to fabricate a money-holding device of fine cloth from the aural appendage of a porcine quadruped.

5. When precipitation occurs it has a marked tendency to do so in excessive quantities.

ANSWER NO.172

PUZZLE 99

How well do you know stage musicals, old and new? Below you'll find some of them with their vowels missing. Can you work out what the musicals should be?

1. PHNTM F TH PR
2. CRSL
3. VT
4. STRLGHT XPRSS
5. TH SND F MSC
6. LS MSRBLS
7. CHSS
8. MSS SGN
9. RCKY HRRR SHW
10. CTS

 ANSWER NO.68

PUZZLE 100

This fairy tale character was a bit of a bird brain.
Maybe that's how she got so confused.

LEVEL C

ANSWER NO.155

Can you find the ten movies hidden in the passage below?

I often visit my cousin on a Friday afternoon. On this particular occasion she was doodling on a piece of green card when I arrived. I couldn't be sure (she's not exactly famous for her artistic talents!) but her drawing seemed to be of a group of gorillas. In the mist outside her window I could just make out her dog frolicking in the flowerbeds.

As was her custom, my cousin made me a cup of tea. I don't know about you, but I can't drink tea until it's cooled off a bit. Some like it hot, but I'm certainly not one of them!

"Who's that girl?" I inquired, pointing at a photograph that was perched on top of her television.

"That's Hannah – and her sisters are in the other photo over there. Hannah's a mannequin – it's a wonderful life for her, you know. In the world of fashion modelling she's a real star.

Wars may happen, natural disasters change the face of the earth as we know it , but Hannah will always be a success. By contrast, her sisters do little – women, they believe, shouldn't leave the kitchen sink."

ANSWER NO.49

PUZZLE 102

The words below spell out four well-known phrases. The first word of each line is in the right place but the others have been mixed up so that, although the word is in the right place within a line, it has been moved up or down and is now in the wrong line. You have to sort them out. To help you there is a clue for each line.

The	does	and	Pooh	king
The	huff	at	future	puff
How	house	your	I'll	Corner
I'll	once	and	garden	grow

Clues:
- Line 1. King Arthur
- Line 2. Christopher Robin
- Line 3. Contrary Gardener
- Line 4. Big Bad threat

ANSWER NO.58

PUZZLE 103

The following are well-known books disguised in newspaper headlines.

GIRL IN RABBIT HOLE DRAMA CLAIMS BIZARRE ADVENTURE

MISSISSIPPI BOY – PRESUMED DEAD – RETURNS WITH TREASURE

TRANSYLVANIAN COUNT WANTED ON ASSAULT CHARGES FLEES TO ENGLAND

MARINER CLAIMS STRANGE ADVENTURE AMONG TINY PEOPLE

SMALL BOY IN MOUSE TRANSFORMATION. SHOCKING WITCHCRAFT ALLEGATION

ANSWER NO.86

PUZZLE 104

Here are some more proverbs disguised with pompous phrasing and long words. Simplify!

1. Everything which reflects sparkling brilliance is not necessarily composed of a precious, malleable, ductile metallic element.

2. A concretion of mineral matter incessantly turning upon its surface is extremely unlikely to acquire a collection of small primitive plants.

3. Herbage always appears to have a more intense shade of verdancy when it is seen upon the far side of a boundary marker.

4. In order to apprehend someone who misappropriates the property of others it is necessary to retain the services of a person engaged in the same profession.

5. It is a strange fact that vexatious circumstances always appear to arrive as triplets.

ANSWER NO.111

PUZZLE 105

Can you work out what these proverbs are supposed to be?
One word of each proverb can be found in each column.

Too	stitch	rains	but	it	day
A	many	built	feather	a	broth
It	wasn't	cooks	in	flock	pours
Rome	of	a	time	saves	together
Birds	never	in	spoil	the	nine

ANSWER NO.13

PUZZLE 106

Here are some book titles in which all the consonants have been removed. Can you work out the titles just from the vowels? It's rather difficult, so we've given a clue to each one.

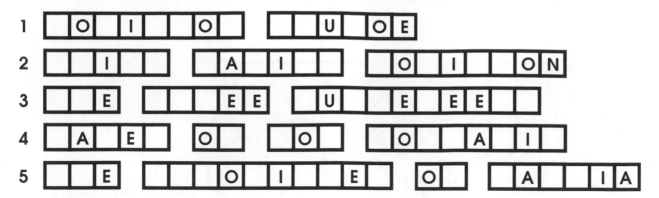

1. `_ O _ I _ _ O _   _ _ U _ O E`
2. `_ _ I _ _ A _ I _   _ _ O _ I _ O N`
3. `_ _ E _ _ _ E E _ U _ _ E _ E E _`
4. `_ A _ E _ _ O _ _ O _ _ O _ A _ I`
5. `_ _ E _ _ _ O _ I _ E _ O _ A _ I A`

1. Desert Island.
2. Another island, same name!
3. All for one!
4. Hobbit friend
5. Aslan

ANSWER NO.104

PUZZLE 107

What is the musical instrument hidden in the riddle?

My first is in **PROMISE**, but not in **PRIZE**

My second's in **ACTOR**, but not **COMPROMISE**

My third is in **EXCELLENCE**, but not in **OVER**

My fourth is in **ORANGE**, and also in **CLOVER**

My fifth is in **SLOPE**, but not in **GREASE**

My sixth is in **SHELF**, but not in **PEACE**

My seventh's in **POLITE**, and also in **POINT**

My eighth is in **TONGUE**, and also **ANOINT**

My ninth is in **GRAPE**, but not in **GONG**

And here is the end of my silly song!

ANSWER NO.130

PUZZLE 108

The words on the scales of the monster are an anagram of a
dinosaur name though, needless to say, it is not the one pictured.
Can you work out which big beast is hidden in the puzzle?

HEAD BANGERS

★ LEVEL D ★

PUZZLE 109

If you add the same letter to the end of the left word and the start of the right one on each line, you will find the name of a famous film star reading down. Who is he?

STAR	?	WINE
CELL	?	MISSION
FAR	?	ASK
AMNESIA	?	REST
ANGLE	?	AFTER
MEN	?	NIT
CHILL	?	SLAM
TUB	?	HOE
SHIN	?	BONY

ANSWER NO.147

PUZZLE 110

My first is in TIGER, but not in CAT
My second's in UGLY, but not ACROBAT
My next is in UMBRELLA, and also in BELL
My fourth is in OWL, but not in JEWEL
My fifth and my fourth are two peas in a pod
My whole is a dwelling that some may find odd

❬?❭ANSWER NO.162❬?❭

PUZZLE 111

The names of three creatures often found as pets have been mixed up.
All the letters are in the right order.

D G O
O
R A G
L
D B B
F
I I T S
H

❬?❭ ANSWER NO.22 ❬?❭

The following figures, representing certain letters, make up a ten letter word:

1   2   3   4   5   6   7   8   9   10

Your task is to work out the above word by making use of the clues below.

4 2 10 6   *means* a list specifying a fixed order

5 2 9 10 4 8 7   *means* part of the nose

7 6 8 4   *means* a lion's home

1 2 3 9 10   *means* combat on horseback

ANSWER NO.40

PUZZLE 113

Below you'll find the names of five birds which all start from the central C.
The letters which make up the words are connected vertically, horizontally and diagonally.
Not every letter is used and some may be used more than once. What are the birds?

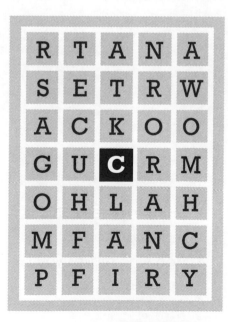

ANSWER NO.75

LEVEL D

PUZZLE 114

The unpronounceable jumbles below are really States in America without their vowels.
How many of them can you unravel?

CLFRN DH NBRSK HW LSK

ANSWER NO.93

PUZZLE 115

All the answers to the clues below are five-letter words.
When you have written them in the grid, you will be able to read the names
of two signs of the zodiac down the first and last columns. Which ones?

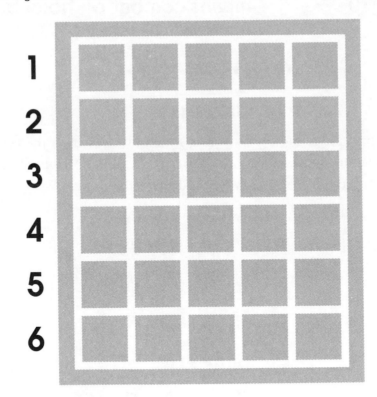

1. To move around quietly
2. Someone who says you were with them when the crime was committed.
3. You have these on fingers and toes.
4. Man who makes you laugh as his job.
5. Bird of prey.
6. A train runs on these.

ANSWER NO.4

PUZZLE 116

All the words in the left-hand box have something in common. Which of the words in the right-hand box should join them?

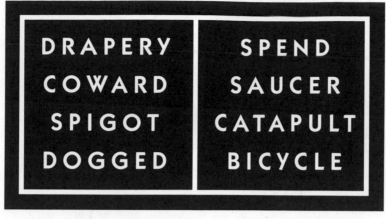

DRAPERY	SPEND
COWARD	SAUCER
SPIGOT	CATAPULT
DOGGED	BICYCLE

ANSWER NO.119

PUZZLE 117

Below are ten clues. To help you we've supplied the consonants for each answer.

1. Not straightforward

| | B | L | | Q | | | |

2. The unlimited extent of space

| | N | F | | N | | T | Y |

3. Conceit

| | R | R | | G | | N | C | |

4. To recover after sickness

| C | | N | V | | L | | S | C | |

5. A period of 1000 years

| M | | L | L | | N | N | | | M |

6. Having effects below the level of conscious awareness

| S | | B | L | | M | | N | | L |

7. Having human characteristics

| H | | M | | N | | | D |

8. Inventiveness

| | N | G | | N | | | T | Y |

9. Basic

| R | | D | | M | | N | T | | R | Y |

10. A bunch of flowers

| B | | | Q | | | T |

LEVEL D

ANSWER NO.136

PUZZLE 118

As you can see, a shark has been at work. He's chewed up a lot of fish and left their spare syllables scattered on the sea bed. However, you may be able to save the situation by putting the syllables back together again to form the names of five kinds of fish.
Which is the one left over?

DUCK   HAD   CU   DA

BAR   CAT

DOCK

BOM

FISH   PIR

AN   HA

BEL

RA   BAY

ANSWER NO.173

PUZZLE 119

Can you find a nine-letter word scrambled in the square?
Clue: A bit jumpy.

ANSWER NO.69

HEAD BANGERS

PUZZLE 120

Your first task is to solve the clues below. When you have your seven answers, you'll find these letters also contain the names of five breeds of dog. Which breeds?

CLUES

GREAT JOY AND HIGH SPIRITS _ _ _ _ _ _ _

EVERYTHING _ _ _

A PIECE OF INCLINED GROUND _ _ _ _ _

SPAGHETTI IS AN EXAMPLE OF THIS _ _ _ _ _

HUE OFTEN ASSOCIATED WITH ROSES _ _ _

TO MAKE SOMEONE A PRIEST _ _ _ _ _ _

AN OBJECT WHICH SEPARATES _ _ _ _ _ _ _

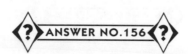 ANSWER NO.156

ANSWER NO.156

LEVEL D

PUZZLE 121

Here are 40 sets of three letters. Using each set only once and without changing the order of the letters can you make 20 six-letter English words?

ora	can	joc	bas	mis	ver	plu	hap	ous	dam
gin	sen	fix	nor	ius	por	law	cud	wig	age
pen	out	suf	fam	qua	ear	ket	ral	try	key
mal	dle	ang	sel	voy	lay	gen	did	ter	mar

 ANSWER NO.48

ANSWER NO.48

PUZZLE 122

Each line in the rhyme below gives one letter of a well-known city.
Can you work out the identity of this ten-letter European capital?

My first is in TRACE, but not in PLAN

My second's in ROTTEN, but not in MILAN

My third is in PORTRAIT, but not in SUNRISE

My fourth is in PRETTY, and also SURPRISE

My fifth is in FRIEND, but not in COMPARE

My sixth is in GHETTO, but not in DESPAIR

My seventh's in DECADE, and also in DAMP

My eighth is in GINGER, but not in REVAMP

My ninth is in GOVERN, and also in NIECE

My tenth is in LANGUAGE, but is not in CEASE.

ANSWER NO.57

PUZZLE 123

How may words of three letters or more can you find in this square?
The computer found 102, but as you don't have a microchip in your head we don't expect
you to get quite so many! A score of fifteen is good, twenty-five very good and forty or
more excellent. What is the nine letter word?

ANSWER NO.87

PUZZLE 124

Which of the following can be seen at some time in the night sky, with a telescope if necessary?

URSA MAJOR   BETELGEUSE

ORION   COPERNICUS

CUMULUS   ANTARCTICA

HORSE NEBULA   PLUTO

JOHN MAJOR   CASCARA

NEPTUNE   PERSEIDS

VENUS   HALLEY'S COMET

HADES   DOMESTICA

ANSWER NO.110

LEVEL D

PUZZLE 125

Below you'll find some anagrams of well-known people. Can you work out who they are?

1. **G's huge bore** (American politician)

2. **C Kindles Search** (English writer)

3. **Moodier Me** (Actress)

4. **Shy without neon** (Singer)

5. **A new antic – So?** (Inventor)

ANSWER NO.12

PUZZLE 126

Take a letter from each country in turn to make another 7 letter country.
Clue: It could feel a little chilly here!

```
I   R   E   L   A   N   D
A   M   E   R   I   C   A
G   E   R   M   A   N   Y
F   I   N   L   A   N   D
A   U   S   T   R   I   A
D   E   N   M   A   R   K
E   N   G   L   A   N   D
```

ANSWER NO.105

PUZZLE 127

Look carefully at the following 'words'. If you replace the numbers with
Roman numerals you should be able to read them easily.

1000 o 500 1 100 u 1000

100 a 500 1000 1 u 1000

a 100 a 500 e 1000 1 100

500 u 1000 1000 1 e 500

a 100 100 e 500 e 500

ANSWER NO.131

PUZZLE 128

Reading down, the name of a well-known young actress should be revealed in the middle column which is currently empty. To discover her identity, it is useful for you to know that each letter of her name will help you create two brand new words on every line, the left one ending with the letter, the right one starting. Who is she?

HALLO		ASH
SCAMP		DEAL
AWAKE		EON
CAME		WE
ARISE		OR
ARE		KIN
PEA		EACH
BUS		OWL
JOSTLE		ARK
HOP		VENT
STRANGE		ANKLE

ANSWER NO.30

D LEVEL D

PUZZLE 129

The jumble of letters below contains five three-letter words. Each is the name of a living creature. The letters are in different type styles but always in the same order. The order is:

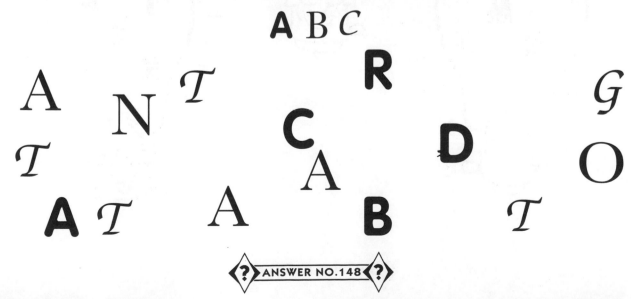

ANSWER NO.148

PUZZLE 130

There are five five-letter words hidden in the light bulbs.
Take a letter from each bulb to find them.
They have all something to do with light.

ANSWER NO.161

PUZZLE 131

If you cut letters in half horizontally it is much easier to recognise the top half than the bottom. For that reason all the words below are made up from – you guessed! – bottom halves. To help you, all the words are types of food.

◇?◇ ANSWER NO.21 ◇?◇

PUZZLE 132

The names of two animals are hidden in each of the sentences below.
Can you find them?

1. A dynamo used by a mad scientist will endanger billionaires.

2. On her job application form she epitomised all the qualities they required.

3. Noah's tendency to cherish arks was perfectly understandable.

4. William wants to grab bits of gossip like him, do you abhor secrecy.

5. Peering through the uncommon keyhole he learnt of plans of their brilliant elopement.

6. He would like to go to Moscow but she insists on Budapest.

7. His bravado gave us a false impression: indeed the whole thing's a sham, sternness being our best reaction.

8. I prefer athletics, although the commentator's waffle annoys me.

◇?◇ ANSWER NO.39 ◇?◇

LEVEL D

PUZZLE 133

Below you can see a number of syllables in alphabetical order and a list of clues. All the answers to the clues can be made from combinations of the syllables given. Each syllable is used ONCE only. When you have solved all the clues, the first letters should give you the name of a well-known fictional character.

A   AL   AP   BRA   DI   DOUG   EM   GE   GO   IN   IT
JE   LA   LAS   LE   LEM   LY   MARE   MI   NA   NEP   NIGHT
ON   OR   OS   PER   PLE   PO   RU   SA   SA   TRICH   TUNE

CLUES

EUROPEAN COUNTRY (5)	FRUIT (5)	FLIGHTLESS BIRD (7)
FRENCH EMPEROR (8)	DREAM (9)	PLANET (7)
BOY'S NAME (6)	BRANCH OF MATHEMATICS (7)	SUPREME RULER (7)
COLOUR OF THE RAINBOW (6)	HOLY CITY (9)	SAUSAGE (6)

 ANSWER NO.92

PUZZLE 134

The grid contains some letters to help you. Use the clues to fill in the missing letters and you will find a word written along the body of the snake.

A			E		D	Go up
		T		L		Fight
	R				A	Middle East
C		E				Saucy
		O		Z		Metal
E			L			Large birds of prey
	R			I		Frozen north
	O		G			Branches

ANSWER NO.3

PUZZLE 135

The leaves of the tree contain groups of letters which, when unscrambled, will give you the names of five types of tree. What are they?

ANSWER NO.118

LEVEL D

PUZZLE 136

Look at the words on this moon map.
They form an anagram of a well known lunar feature.

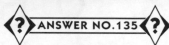

ANSWER NO.135

PUZZLE 137

Danny Diablo has gone on a school outing to the art gallery. His teacher prayed that, for once, he would be good but within minutes of entering the building he has switched round the names of several famous artists. Can you rearrange them before the warder notices and throws the whole class out?

VINCENT   CHAGALL

LEONARDO   PICASSO

PABLO   CONSTABLE

JOHN   DA VINCI

MARC   VAN GOGH

ANSWER NO.174

PUZZLE 138

The words below have some of their letters replaced by symbols. Each symbol always represents the same letter. To help you we have also put in some clues.

Trading before money

Party wind bag

Make

Dealer

Plunderer

Scold harshly

ANSWER NO.70

PUZZLE 139

In each sentence you'll find the name of one sport hidden. Can you locate all six of them?

1. The whole thing was rather a shock, eyebrows being raised in the highest of places.

2. The English aristocracy clings to old values, for it fears a world without them.

3. That really was a bad mint on the whole; it stuck to my teeth like glue.

4. Her horrid ingratitude was beyond belief, and she was sent to bed without supper.

5. My cat will attack a rat every time.

6. He started making loud jokes in order to mask a tingling in his left foot.

ANSWER NO.157

LEVEL D

PUZZLE 140

Along the arms of the tentacles of the octopus you will see the names of marine creatures disguised in a special way. How many can you catch?

TEETH GRINDERS

★ LEVEL E ★

PUZZLE 141

The seven letter words below are all in code. The same symbol always stands for the same letter. To help you a clue is given at the end of each line and two letters have been left uncoded.

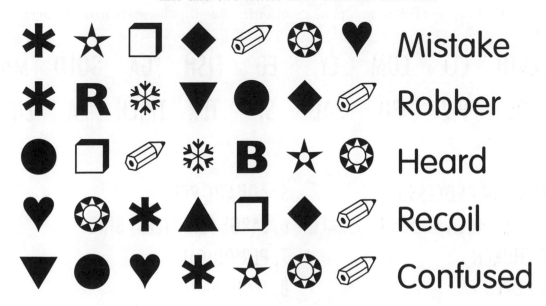

ANSWER NO.56

PUZZLE 142

The following sentence is missing three words which are anagrams of each other. Each dash represents a missing letter. What are the words?

The _ _ _ _ _ _ said that I was a _ _ _ _ _ _ _ because I had the word _ _ _ _ _ _ written on my hand in the spelling test.

ANSWER NO.88

PUZZLE 143

The answers to the clues below can be found in the list of syllables. However, all the syllables have been presented in alphabetical order. See if you can rearrange them.

BI   CATH   CLE   COM   CY   ED   FISH   GA   GOLD   MA

NAI   OS   PIZ   PU   RAL   SI   TER   TRICH   ZA   ZINE

CLUES
1. INFORMATION PROCESSOR
2. WILDERNESS AREA SOUTH OF ISRAEL
3. LARGE CHURCH
4. ITALIAN OPEN PIE

5. AQUATIC PET
6. LARGE FLIGHTLESS BIRD
7. PERIODICAL
8. CONVEYANCE

ANSWER NO.109

PUZZLE 144

The following eight-letter words have been coded using Greek style letters.
Even if you don't know any Greek you will be able to work out the words
if you use the clues we have given.

Λ Ξ Φ Γ Λ Μ Ε Τ   HANDBONES

Δ Φ Γ Λ Μ Ι Ξ Η   BABY DUCK

Ι Ξ Λ Μ Ι Ξ Η Τ   VAGUE IDEAS

Π Ι Γ Λ Μ Ι Ξ Η   PRESERVING FOOD

Ι Ξ Γ Μ Φ Δ Ε Τ   CONTAINS

 ANSWER NO.11

PUZZLE 145

The following sentences have been de-punctuated to turn them into nonsense.
Can you add punctuation to make them grammatical?
Each is not necessarily a single sentence.

**1. She said that that that that I said should
have been those**

**2. The culprit made his admission sorrowfully
the day after he was shot**

**3. I said and but he said I said but but he
was wrong and I said so**

 ANSWER NO.106

LEVEL E

PUZZLE 146

The words in the box have something in common.
Which of the following words should join them?

cup
group
proud
buds
jogs

kill

then

bugs

ANSWER NO.132

PUZZLE 147

The following groups of words are all proverbs in which the words
have been jumbled up. How many can you work out?

1 And many between cup there's slip a lip

2 They count before your hatch chickens don't

3 Judge cover by its never a book

4 Most vessels make empty noise

5 Be out find your sure sin will you

ANSWER NO.29

PUZZLE 148

A rebus is a word, phrase or saying cunningly hidden in a illustration.

Here are a few to try.

1 JUST

2 c l o u d

3 IS

4 SHIP

5 THING THING

6 STEP   STEP

7 VIOLINIST

8
THE
RESORT
RESORT
RESORT
RESORT

9
PIGGY
PIGGY
PIGGY

10
WHECAS
ZALIRB
TAWLUN
CANPE

11 YOUNG

12 S E A L

13
| 1 2 3 4 5 6 7 8 9 10 11 12 |
ROOST

◆? ANSWER NO.149 ?◆

LEVEL E

PUZZLE 149

The answers to the clues below are syllables which, when rearranged,
will make the names of five countries. To help you,
there's a hint to the identity of the syllables in brackets after each clue.

A stain or blot (rhymes with 'spark')   **The first letter of the alphabet**

Me (rhymes with 'pie')   (rhymes with 'pay')

An old fashioned girl's name   **Some** (rhymes with 'penny')

(rhymes with 'wader')   **Part of the face** (rhymes with 'bin')

Home of a predatory animal   **A tin for food** (rhymes with 'man')

(rhymes with 'when')   **Past tense of run** (rhymes with 'fan')

Common name for the thing which causes illness (rhymes with 'worm')

ANSWER NO.160

PUZZLE 150

Can you fill in these blanks? In each puzzle the letters
missing are the same for every line.

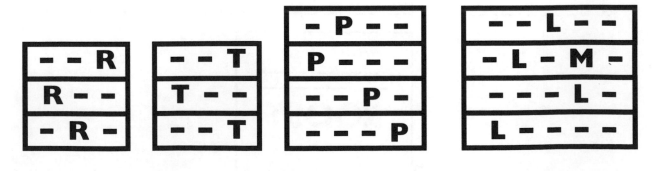

ANSWER NO.20

PUZZLE 151

Using the letters we have given you and the clues on the right fill in the missing letters.
When you have finished you will find there is a word running down the snake.

		G			Finger
			N		Thousands of Years
		C			Desert plants
				K	Hit
		O			Tree Seed
A					Pains
	L				Another name
			S		Happiness
	E				Greek Island

ANSWER NO.38

ANSWER NO.38

PUZZLE 152

Can you unravel these ten words? The clues in brackets could help you,
as they mean the same as the scrambled words.

1. **EITDRVNE**
(back to front)

2. **DAEOFHLSO**
(lie)

3. **VLICARUSHO**
(gallant)

4. **ASDEHFMI**
(starving)

5. **HIANVS**
(disappear)

6. **REOMET**
(shooting star)

7. **LHEROCT**
(laugh)

8. **UPSSEO**
(husband)

9. **CARCIEP**
(whim)

10. **ETRPMEITD**
(allowed)

ANSWER NO.73

PUZZLE 153

The words in the box have been chosen according to a simple system.
Can any of the words outside join them.

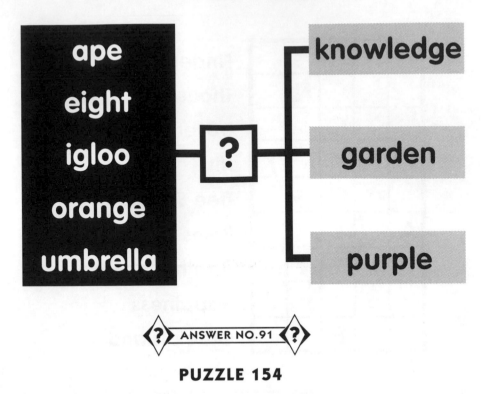

ape
eight
igloo
orange
umbrella

?

knowledge

garden

purple

? ANSWER NO.91 ?

PUZZLE 154

In each of the five sentences below two numbers are hiding.
It is your task to seek them out.

1. Bridget went yesterday, anxious even though we had reassured her she would be alright.

2. At the windmill I once played my accordion every day.

3. Keith reeled in surprise as the horse's sudden neigh threw him into confusion.

4. He was left woefully short of cash, having been spending again in excess of what he could truly afford.

5. The scheme was foolproof, our accountant encouraged us to start immediately.

? ANSWER NO.2 ?

PUZZLE 155

Use the clues to fill in the missing words and complete the snail. To help you you'll find that the last letter of each word must be used as the first letter of the next word. The number of letters for each answer is given at the end of the clue.

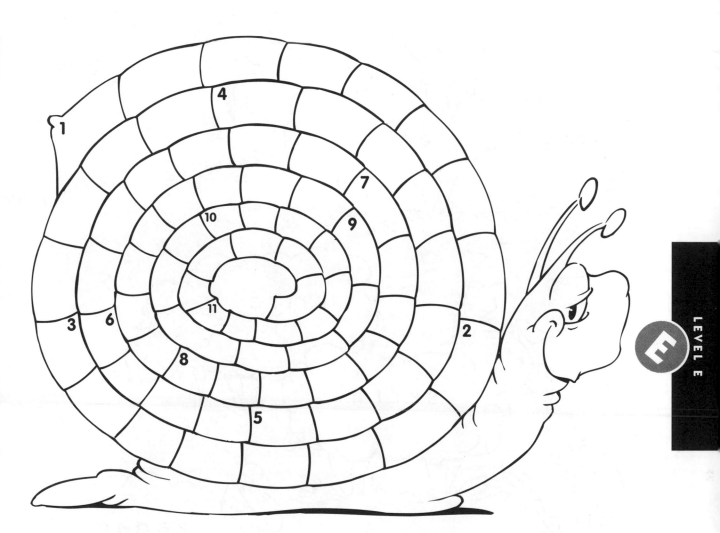

1. Pay this in class or teacher won't be pleased (9)

2. This is most of the air we breath (8)

3. Lump of gold (6)

4. You can bear it – just about! (9)

5. Weird (5)

6. Aubergine (8)

7. The hare will always beat him in the race (8)

8. The person who saw the crime (10)

9. A noisy quarrel (8)

10. Getting the chop at dawn! (9)

11. Zero (7)

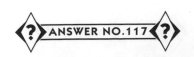 ANSWER NO.117

LEVEL E

PUZZLE 156

Take a letter from each animal and make five
six-letter words connected with farms.

1

ANSWER NO.134

PUZZLE 157

Here we have mixed the names of trees with the names of places where people live. See if you can untangle the resulting strange words.

PALBEAM

HORNACE

CAPLE

MASTLE

GALOWRED

BUNWOOD

MONAR

HICKAGE

COTTORY

CEDASTERY

◇?〉 ANSWER NO.175 〈?◇

PUZZLE 158

The words around the circle can be rearranged to form the name of a country.

Clue: 51

ADAMANT CERTIFIES TO USE

◇?〉 ANSWER NO.71 〈?◇

PUZZLE 159

Complete the phrases below, then write the missing words in the grid
with the first letter in the box. You should be able to read a six-letter word down.

Clue: Fish

_ _ _ jump

_ _ _ _ site

_ _ _ _ storm

_ _ _ _ _ wave

_ _ _ _ _ days

_ _ _ _ _ badge

ANSWER NO.158

PUZZLE 160

Change the top word into the bottom one by altering a letter each time
and forming a new word with each move.

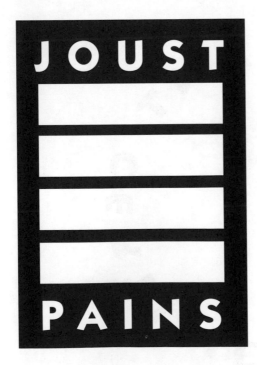

ANSWER NO.46

PUZZLE 161

Match the following words with their position on the body shown.

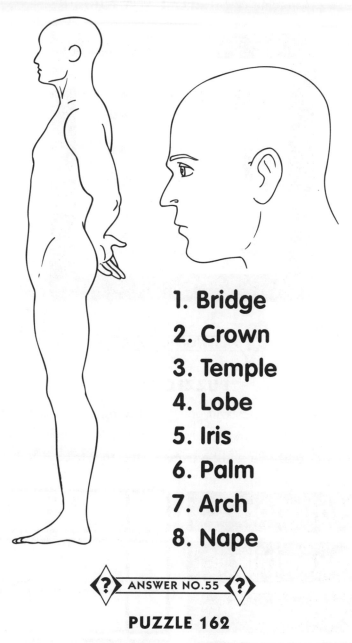

1. **Bridge**
2. **Crown**
3. **Temple**
4. **Lobe**
5. **Iris**
6. **Palm**
7. **Arch**
8. **Nape**

⟨?⟩ ANSWER NO.55 ⟨?⟩

PUZZLE 162

Below you will see thirty syllables. If you rearrange them you'll find that, using each syllable only once, they will make up ten three-syllable words. What are the words?

DI	MAN	TEER	PA	SUS	TUDE	GAST	IN	REAU	DO
SION	AB	NANCE	VER	PER	CATE	GI	BU	BER	UN
TIC	NEWS	LON	DI	RO	VOL	FLAB	MEN	CRAT	TE

⟨?⟩ ANSWER NO.89 ⟨?⟩

PUZZLE 163

Use all the letters in the grid twice to give you two nine-letter words.
The clue is: SILENT LADY KILLERS

❖?❖ ANSWER NO.108 ❖?❖

PUZZLE 164

The following clues will give you the name of six sports.
Read the first letters of the words in order
and you will be transported to Africa.

Natation		
Toxophily		
Soccer		
Track & Field		
Equestrianism		
Blade Balance		

❖?❖ ANSWER NO.10 ❖?❖

PUZZLE 165

Which of the words in the right-hand column can join the left?

ABUNDANT	ELEPHANT
BLOATED	SARACEN
LEGGY	BLIZZARD
STEAM	SCORNED
SCREAMED	NEWT

ANSWER NO.107

PUZZLE 166

Below you will find some clues. We have given you the answers as well!
So where's the puzzle? Well, the answers have been broken into syllables arranged
in alphabetical order. All you have to do is select the right syllables to
answer each clue. Easy! Or is it?

1. AMERICAN UNIVERSITY

2. CAPITAL OF THAILAND

3. COMMON NAME OF PLANT RANUNCULUS

4. ANIMAL WHICH CARRIES ITS YOUNG
   IN A POUCH

5. GAMBLING GAME INVOLVING WHEEL

6. VERY HARD CRYSTALLINE CARBON

7. TREES WHICH LOOSE THEIR
   LEAVES IN WINTER

8. CALEDONIA

9. EATER OF ITS OWN KIND

10. PART OF OUR GALAXY

A	AL	BANG	BUT	CAN	CUP	DEC	DI	ET
HAR	IAL	ID	KOK	LAND	LETTE	MAR	MOND	NIB
OUS	PLAN	ROU	SCOT	SUP	TER	U	VARD	

ANSWER NO.133

LEVEL E

AAARGH!

★ **LEVEL F** ★

PUZZLE 167

The letters below can be fitted into the grid so that they give three
words reading across and one down the middle.

PBTTFAYCUSDEANRA

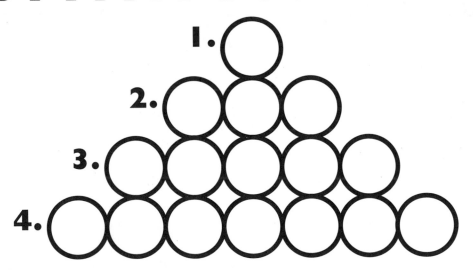

1. **Single letter vegetable**   3. **Well again**

2. **Nocturnal flying animal**   4. **Imagination**

PUZZLE 168

Five of the words below are related in some way. Discover which ones they are
and see if brass could join them.

cease

hares

sloth

beach

again

brown

abbey

frown

green

beans

acids

drama

ANSWER NO.193

LEVEL F

F

PUZZLE 169

Turn the anagrams below into four classic works of English literature.
Name the authors too. Clue: there is a hint to the theme of the books in the anagram.

1. MASK PLAN FIRED

2. SITED HARM

3. MAULED TO REJOIN

4. BOSS DEFILER V THE LUSTRE

ANSWER NO.159

PUZZLE 170

Look at the following list of words. There is something special about them.
Can you work out what it is?

HOAX   THAW   AVOW

IOTA   ATOM   TAXI

MIAOW

 ANSWER NO.192

PUZZLE 171

Look at the signpost below. The distances given are related, by some form
of twisted logic, to the place names. Can you work out the logic and then replace the
question mark with the correct distance? If you want a clue, remember the words
have consonants and vowels.

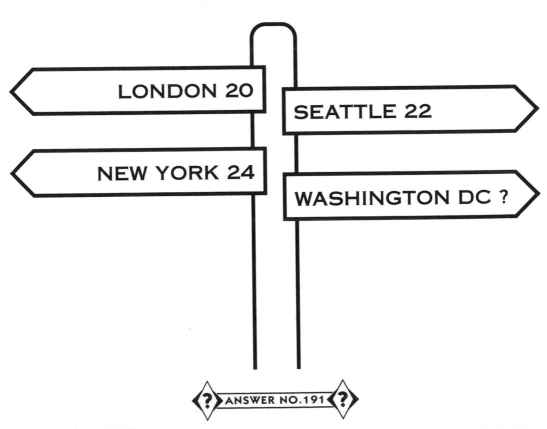

LONDON 20

SEATTLE 22

NEW YORK 24

WASHINGTON DC ?

ANSWER NO.191

AAARGH! F

PUZZLE 172

The clues will help you to find ten hidden words all to do with cycling. The words may be written in any direction and the grid contains dummy letters.

A	X	M	I	R	R	O	R	H
B	E	L	D	D	A	S	B	A
W	I	L	R	T	V	E	S	N
P	O	C	E	T	L	S	E	D
E	E	U	Y	L	J	B	K	L
M	E	D	S	C	A	L	O	E
A	G	W	A	N	L	M	P	B
R	E	V	Q	L	R	E	S	A
F	N	I	A	H	C	T	Y	R
D	R	A	U	G	D	U	M	S

LEVEL F

1. Reflector
2. Steering device
3. Wheel parts
4. Foot rest
5. Driver
6. Splash preventor
7. Seat
8. Ringer
9. Bike
10. Skeleton

ANSWER NO.37

PUZZLE 173

AAARGH! F

ACROSS

1. Tall pole on a ship which supports the sail (4)
6. A person who has no parents (6)
8. Father (2)
9. Part of something (4)
10. It helps you to draw straight lines (5)
12. Tea, lemonade and orange juice are these (6)
13. To carry out something (2)
14. This would be steep to walk up (6)
16. A male deer (4)
18. You use this on your hair to make it stay in place (3)
19. A baby horse (4)
21. You open and close this (4)
23. A narrow passageway (8)

DOWN

1. The early part of the day (7)
2. I am, you – – – (3)
3. A flash (5)
4. A type of bird (6)
5. An outlaw (6)
7. You use this to mend your clothes (6)
11. You fasten this in your hair to make it curl (6)
15. An eskimo's home (5)
16. Water in a plant (3)
17. As well (4)
19. A long way (3)
20. To unite by addition (3)
22. Either, – – (2)

ANSWER NO.72

PUZZLE 174

The letters on the computer screen form a series. What letter replaces the question mark?

OTTFF
SSEN?

?‹ ANSWER NO.90 ›?

PUZZLE 175

Can you work out where these people live?
Fit the names correctly into the boxes and you should have your answer!

4 letters	5 letters	6 letters	7 letters	9 letters	11 letters
Andy	Clare	Amanda	Mrs Hall	Catherine	Miss Coomber
Mary	Sarah		Shelley	Miss Cooke	Mrs Tuckwell
Mike	Tessa			Mr Bushell	
Paul					

?‹ ANSWER NO.1 ›?

PUZZLE 176

Five of the words below are related. Discover which ones they are and then see if confidence could join them.

anteater
encyclopedia
ahead
astrology
red
confederation
hopeless
acrimony
eagles
nausea
acids
telephone
sight
azalea

ANSWER NO.190

PUZZLE 177

The editor's going to be after me. A number puzzle in a word puzzle book! Whatever next? But no, I assure you this is a word puzzle. Why are some numbers above the line?

$$\frac{12 \qquad 6 \qquad 10}{345 \qquad 789}$$

ANSWER NO.184

PUZZLE 178

Start at the top left corner and fill in the answers to the clues, working round the grid in a spiral. The last two letters of each answer form the first two of the next. The number of letters in each answer is given in brackets after the clue.

1				2			3		4
12							13		
					19				
11	18							14	5
						24			
		23							
10	17		25				15		
		22	21			20			
			16						6
	9		8			7			

LEVEL F

1. Capital of UK (6)
2. Vegetable (5)
3. One time only (4)
4. Stop completely (5)
5. Quite a few (7)
6. Permit (5)
7. Possessor (5)
8. Rub out (5)
9. Older (6)
10. Command (5)
11. Historical periods (4)
12. Study of the stars (9)
13. Gold, Frankincense and – – – – – (5)
14. Words with similar endings (eg. Prime time) (5)
15. Given by the Doctor (8)
16. Uneasy (7)
17. Everyday (5)
18. Boy with magic lamp (7)
19. Not seen (9)
20. Citrus fruit (5)
21. Single unit (3)
22. More recent (5)
23. Wipe out completely (9)
24. Extreme fear (6)
25. Groups of fruit trees (8)

ANSWER NO.2

PUZZLE 179

Your task here is to work out which letter of the alphabet is represented by each of the numbers 1 to 26. To help you, we've given you a few letters to start you off. When you work out what the numbers represent, write them in the reference grid at the bottom. The completed puzzle will look like a filled-in crossword, featuring only genuine words.

		8			22	16	10	6	4	7	4	3
25	8	11	11	6		8		16		21	7	
7		7		16		10			14		21	11
26	7	4	21		1		22	24	15	11		23
7			7		4	11			7			9
4			18	16	16		9	6	22	5		6
9	20	24	11		26				13	9	6	
	11			10	9	2	5	6		12		16
	8		2	7	6	11			17	11	7	20
				21		10	7	9	24			20
7	4	6		11		6			15		9	
	7		16			24		12	11	25	6	
	19	15	10	2	24	11				16		

AAARGH! **F**

1	2	3	4 R	5	6 T	7	8 W	9	10 N	11 E	12	13
14	15	16 O	17	18	19	20	21	22	23	24 L	25	26

❖ ANSWER NO. 76 ❖

PUZZLE 180

Look at the diagrams, crack the logic of the puzzle, and discover the missing letters.

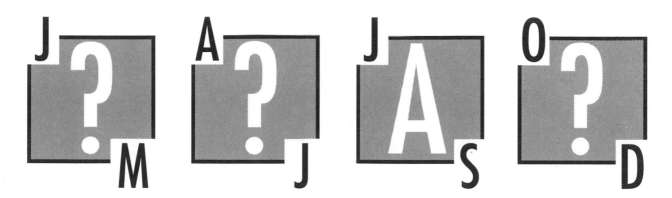

 ANSWER NO.188

PUZZLE 181

Here is part of the menu from Joe's Diner. Joe has his own way of calculating the prices. We're not giving away too many secrets if we tell you it has someting to do with the position of letters in the alphabet. How much does Pizza cost? If you can work it out Joe will give you a free slice.

Joe's Diner

Hamburger $9.30

Cheeseburger $11.60

Hot Dog $6.90

Pizza ...... ?

ANSWER NO.189

PUZZLE 182

In the diagram you see the magic word Abracadabra spelt out as a pyramid. There are various paths from top to bottom but how many ways can you discover to spell the trick word?

A
BB
RRR
AAAA
CCCCC
AAAAAA
DDDDDDD
AAAAAAAA
BBBBBBBBB
RRRRRRRRRR
AAAAAAAAAAA

ANSWER NO.187

PUZZLE 183

Start at the top left square and fill in the answers to the clues.
The LAST TWO letters of each word form the first two letters of the next word.
Follow the grid in an ever-decreasing spiral to the centre.

Grid cell labels: 1, 2, 8, 9, 3, 15, 16, 7, 14, 20, 10, 13, 19, 17, 18, 4, 12, 11, 6, 5

1. Wild dog (6)
2. Water tortoise (8)
3. Discoverer of new ideas (8)
4. Musical instrument (5)
5. Story (8)
6. Used for long distance conversation (9)
7. Worn for decoration (8)
8. Eaten at breakfast (6)
9. Type of maths (7)
10. Demanded by kidnappers (6)

11. Sign to the superstitious (4)
12. Holds a letter (8)
13. Fruit (4)
14. Reach your destination (6)
15. Pest (6)
16. Crazy (6)
17. Closer (6)
18. Mistake (5)
19. Music makers (10)
20. To do with fortune telling using the stars (12)

 ANSWER NO.19

PUZZLE 184

Just a brief message, irritatingly obscure of course.
Can you work it out?

FYTHNKTHSSGNGTBS
YYHDBTTRTHNKAGN

 ANSWER NO.183

PUZZLE 185

Look at the signpost below. The distances given are related, by some form of twisted logic, to the place names. Can you work out the logic and then replace the question mark with the correct distance?

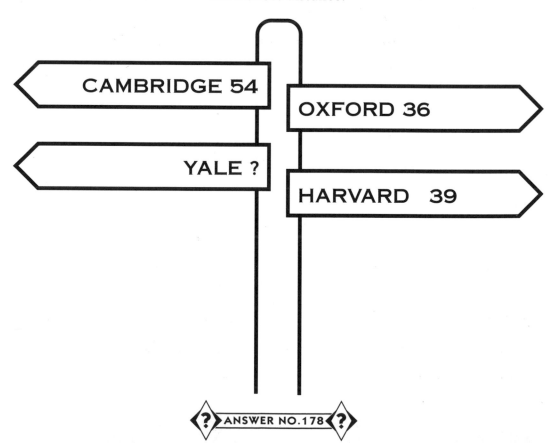

CAMBRIDGE 54

OXFORD 36

YALE ?

HARVARD 39

ANSWER NO.178

PUZZLE 186

The letters in the computer screen make a series.
Work out the logic and replace the question mark.

AEAPAU
UUECO?

? ANSWER NO.150 ?

PUZZLE 187

Five of the words below are related. Discover which ones they are
and then see if heady could join them.

fireball

ready

it

yellow

transubstantiation

hamburger

analysis

anything

bottomless

acolyte

rival

rivet

golf

? ANSWER NO.185 ?

PUZZLE 188

Look at the word below. It's actually Monrovian for 'Mine's a large cheeseburger with extra relish.' No, that's a lie. But the letters do have one strange property. What is it?

EHIKOX

 ANSWER NO. 186

PUZZLE 189

Five of the words below are related. Discover which ones they are and then see if ability could join them.

ziggurat average

ear gizmo

introduction

onomatopoeia

uncle xylophone

classic

hangman

numerical

depend force

grass white

 ANSWER NO. 179

PUZZLE 190

Look at the signpost below. The distances given are related, by some form of twisted logic, to the place names. Can you work out the logic and then replace the question mark with the correct distance?

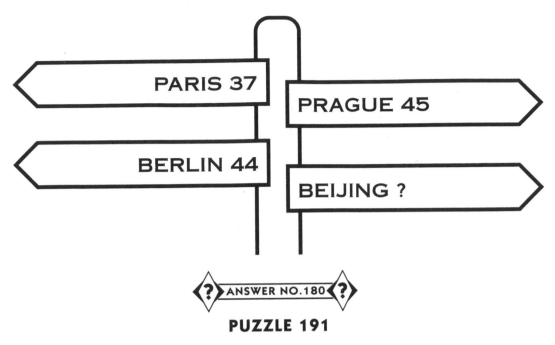

ANSWER NO.180

PUZZLE 191

Too many people knew the code to Joe's menu and he was losing a fortune in free pizza. Now he has a new code (still based on the value of letters). Can you crack it, discover the price of pancakes, and win a free hamburger?

ANSWER NO.182

PUZZLE 192

Look at the signpost below. The distances given are related, by some form of twisted logic, to the place names. Can you work out the logic and then replace the question mark with the correct distance? If you want a clue, remember that words have consonants and vowels.

AAARGH!

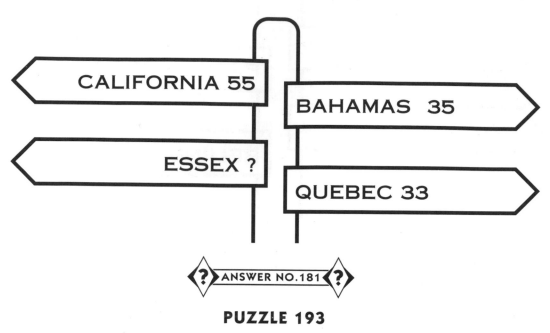

CALIFORNIA 55

BAHAMAS 35

ESSEX ?

QUEBEC 33

? ANSWER NO.181 **?**

PUZZLE 193

Walter is planning a holiday but is not quite sure where he's going.
Can you help him by matching the country to the capital city.

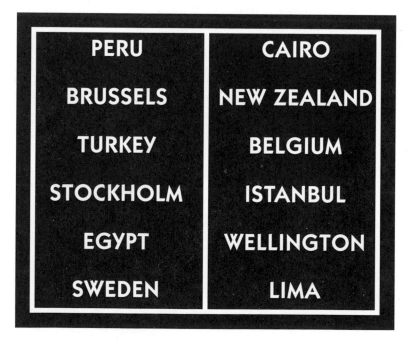

PERU   CAIRO

BRUSSELS   NEW ZEALAND

TURKEY   BELGIUM

STOCKHOLM   ISTANBUL

EGYPT   WELLINGTON

SWEDEN   LIMA

? ANSWER NO.74 **?**

ANSWERS

1

```
Left grid:
        M A R Y
        R
        S
  C A T H E R I N E        M I S S  (COOKE)
  L     U       I
  A     C       S
  R     K       S
  E     W       C
        E       O
        L       O
        L       K
                E

Middle grid:
              M
        S A R A H
              B
        P A U L
              S
  T           H       A
  E           E       N
  S           L       D
  S H E L L E Y       Y
  A

Right grid:
              M I K E
              I
        M R S H A L L
              C       M
              O       A
              O       N
              M       D
              B       A
              E
              R
```

2
1. London.
2. Onion.
3. Once.
4. Cease.
5. Several.
6. Allow
7. Owner.
8. Erase.
9. Senior.
10. Order.
11. Era.
12. Astronomy.
13. Myrrh.
14. Rhyme.
15. Medicine.
16. Nervous.
17. Usual.
18. Aladdin.
19. Invisible.
20. Lemon.
21. One.
22. Newer.
23. Eradicate.
24. Terror.
25. Orchards.

3 Ascend, Battle, Arabia, Cheeky, Bronze, Eagles, Arctic, Boughs. The answer is Strength.

4 Creep, Alibi, Nails, Comic, Eagle, Rails. The signs of the zodiac are Cancer and Pisces.

5 Cinderella.

6 Indigo, Number, Treaty, Race, India, Glue, Umbrella, Elephant. The word is intrigue.

7 John Lennon
Helena Bonham-Carter
Napoleon Bonaparte
Elizabeth Taylor
Neil Armstrong
Albert Einstein
Richard Gere.

8 Horse, Goats, Mules, Sheep, Ducks.

9 Red.

10 Swimming, Archery, Football, Athletics, Riding, Ice skating. The word is Safari.

11 Knuckles, Ducklings, Inklings, Pickling, Includes.

12 George Bush
Charles Dickens
Demi Moore
Whitney Houston
Isaac Newton.

13 Too many cooks spoil the broth.
A stich in time saves nine.
It never rains but it pours.
Rome wasn't built in a day.
Birds of a feather flock together.

14 Little Red Riding Hood.

15 Sonic the Hedgehog.

16 Smell, Maid, Cheap,
Thank, Peace, Flog,
Weld, Beard.
The girl's name is Michelle.

17 Arm, Head, Leg, Foot.

18 Lucy. (Captain Hook,
Peter Pan, Christopher
Robin, Humpty Dumpty,
Mother Goose, Betty
Botter).

19 See below.

20 1. Mar, Ram, Arm.
2. Art, Tar, Rat.
3. Spar, Pars, Raps, Rasp.
4. Miles, Slime, Smile, Limes.

21 Pizza, Chicken, Doughnut, Sandwich, Salad, Ice cream.

22 Dog, Goldfish, Rabbit.

23 Faint heart never won fair lady.
A bird in the hand is worth two in the bush.
Its no use crying over

19

spilt milk.
People who live in glass houses shouldn't throw stones.

24 Fast, Area, Sets, Task.

25 Become. The words start and end with consecutive letters of the alphabet, eg, AdverB, CarD, EngulF, etc.

26 Kirsty. It doesn't have the letter A in it.

27 Apes.

28

```
              P
        B     A     T
    C   U     R     E     D
F   A   N     T     A     S     Y
```

29 There's many a slip between cup and lip.
Don't count your chickens before they hatch.
Never judge a book by it's cover.
Empty vessels make most noise.
Be sure your sin will find you out.

30 Winona Ryder.

31 Tyrannosaurus Rex.

32 Eggs, as all the others are dairy products.
August, as all the others have an 'R' in the month.
Spider, as all the others are insects.
Poland, as all the others are in the European Union.
Nova Scotia, as all the others are in America.
Harley-Davidson, as all the others are cars.
Cambridge, as all the others are rivers.
Cyclone, as all the others are types of cloud.

33 Apple, Norman, Opera, Night, Yellow Mark, Opium, Ugly, Sea.

The word is anonymous.

34 Neigh, Snowy, Ready Thorn, Large.

35 Bulldog, Dogfish.

36 Father Christmas.

37 See over.

38 Digit, Aeons, Cacti, Knock, Acorn, Aches, Alias, Bliss, Crete
The answer is deckchair.

39 1. Mouse and Gerbil.
2. Cat and Sheep.
3. Shark and Wasp.
4. Rabbit and Horse.
5. Monkey and Antelope.
6. Cow and Ape.
7. Dog and Hamster.
8. Rat and Flea.

40 Rota, Nostril, Lair, Joust. The 10 letter word is journalist.

41 Rumplestiltskin.

42 25.

43 Oliver Cromwell
Mahatma Gandhi
George Washington
William Cody
Michelle Pfeiffer
Julia Roberts
Robin Hood.

44 Catherine Wheel.

45 Unbearable.

46 Joust, Joist, Joint, Point, Paint, Pains.
Clock, Cloak, Croak, Creak, Break, Bread.

47 Catfish, Plaice, Marlin, Dolphin, Haddock, Tunny, Squid, Oyster. All vowels are replaced by X.

48 Angora
Basket
Candid
Cuddle

ANSWERS

A	X	M	I	R	R	O	R	H
B	E	L	D	D	A	S	B	A
W	I	L	R	T	V	E	S	N
P	O	C	E	T	L	S	E	D
E	E	U	Y	L	J	B	K	L
M	E	D	S	C	A	L	O	E
A	G	W	A	N	L	M	P	B
R	E	V	Q	L	R	E	S	A
F	N	I	A	H	C	T	Y	R
D	R	A	U	G	D	U	M	S

Damsel
Earwig,
Famous
Genius
Happen,
Jockey
Margin
Mislay,
Normal
Outlaw
Porter
Plural
Quaver
Sentry
Suffix
Voyage.

49 Green Card
Gorillas in the Mist

Some Like it Hot
Who's That Girl?
Hannah and her Sisters
Mannequin
It's a Wonderful Life
Star Wars
Always
Little Women.

50 Chinese, Arabic, Italian,
English, Spanish.

51 And, Bat, Dad, Eat,
Bad, End.

52 Bare/Bear, Hare/Hair,
Hart/Heart, Deer/Dear,
Reed/Read, Beet/Beat.

53 Ran.

54 Pa, Pan, Pane, Panel.

55 See below.

56 Blunder, Brigand, Audible, Rebound, Garbled.

57 Copenhagen.

58 The Once and Future King.
The House at Pooh Corner.
How does your garden grow.
I'll huff and I'll puff.

59 Adhesive, Advise, Advises, Ashes, Aside, Asides, Aide, Aides, Aids, Avid, Dash, Dashes, Dais, Daises, Devise, Devises, Dies, Dish, Dishes, Disease, Diva, Divas, Dive, Dives, Have, Haves, Head, Heads, Heavies, Heave, Heaved, Heaves, Heed, Heeds, Hide, Hides, Hiss, Hissed, Hive, Hies, Hived, Hives, Ease, Eased, Eases, Eaves, Evade, Evades, Eves, Said, Save, Saved, Saves, Sash, Shad, Shade, Shades, Shads, Shave, Shaved, Shaves, Sheave, Sheaved, Sheaves, Shed, Sheds, Shield, Shies, Seas, Seaside, Seeds, Seeds, Sees, Side, Sides, Sieve, Sieved, Sieves, Idea, Ideas, Ides, Vase, Vases, Vied, Vies, Visa, Visas.

60 Portugal, Hungary, Romania, Germany, Greece.

61 E.

62 Vermicelli. This is a food.

63 To be or not to be,
That is the question.
(The first and last letters are removed).

64 Scatter.

65 S. (The first letter of Monday, Tuesday, etc.)

66 Idaho.

67 Journey to the Centre of the Earth.
The Last of the Mohicans.
Twenty Thousand Leagues Under the Sea.
The Little House on the Prairie.
On Her Majesty's Secret Service.

55

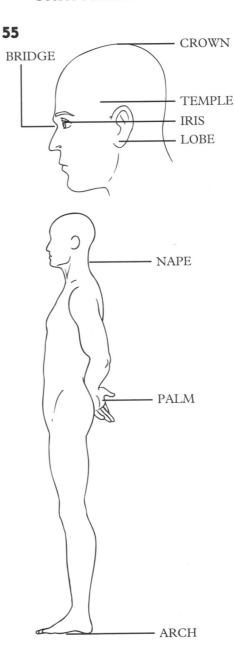

BRIDGE
CROWN
TEMPLE
IRIS
LOBE
NAPE
PALM
ARCH

68
1. Phantom of the Opera.
2. Carousel.
3. Evita.
4. Starlight Express.
5. The Sound of Music.
6. Les Miserables.
7. Chess.
8. Miss Saigon.
9. Rocky Horror Show.
10. Cats.

69 Acrobatic.

70 Barter, Balloon, Create, Trader, Looter, Berate.

71 United States of America.

72 Across
1. Mast
6. Orphan
8. Pa
9. Rear
10. Ruler
12. Drinks
13. Do
14. Hill
16. Stag
18. Gel
19. Foal
21. Door
23. Corridor.

Down
1. Morning
2. Are
3. Spark
4. Thrush
5. Bandit
7. Needle
11. Roller
15. Igloo
16. Sap
17. Also
19. Far
20. Add
22. Or.

73
1. Inverted
2. Falsehood
3. Chivalrous
4. Famished
5. Vanish
6. Meteor
7. Chortle
8. Spouse
9. Caprice
10. Permitted

74 Peru, Lima
New Zealand, Wellington
Belgium, Brussels
Turkey, Istanbul
Sweden, Stockholm
Egypt, Cairo.

75 Cormorant
Crow
Cuckoo
Chaffinch
Canary.

76 See next page.

77 Back.

78 Andre Agassi.

79 Aches.

80 The correct order is omen, pole, fork, knee.
The word is moon.

81 The correct order is shop, away need, down.
Sand is found on the beach.

82 Read down the eighth column from the left, the first letter is on the third line.

83 Settler, Letters.

84 Show and Sow
Open and Pen
Front and Font
Insane and Inane
Fear and Far
Cap and Carp
Neat and Net
Damp and Amp
Rain and Ran
Pest and Pet
Chop and Cop.
Sauce: Horseradish.

85 Money, Honey, Phoney, Phone, Home, Hole, Mole.

86
1. Alice in Wonderland.
2. Tom Sawyer.
3. Dracula.
4. Gulliver's Travels.
5. The Witches.

1 P	2 G	3 Y	4 R	5 H	6 T	7 A	8 W	9 I	10 N	11 E	12 V	13 K
14 Q	15 U	16 O	17 B	18 Z	19 J	20 D	21 M	22 C	23 X	24 L	25 S	26 F

87 Bob, Bobs, Bobsleigh, Bosh, Bole, Boles, Boil, Boils, Bog, Bogs, Bogie, Bogies, Blob, Blobs, Beg, Begs, Bib, Bibs, Bible, Bibles, Bile, Bilge, Big, Oblige, Obliges, Obeli, Oil, Oils Ogle, Ogles, Ohs, Sob, Sol, Sole, Soli, Soil, Soh, Slob, Sloe, Slog, Sleigh, Silo, Sigh, Shoe She, Lob, Lobbies, Lobs, Lobe, Lobes, Lose, Log, Logs, Loge, Loges, Lei, Leis, Leg, Legs, Lib, Lie, Lies, Ebb, Ebbs, Ego, Egos, Isle, Gob, Gobs, Gobble, Gobbles, Goch, Goes, Glob, Globs, Globe, Globes, Glib, Gel, Gels, Gib, Gibboxe, Gibs, Gibe, Gibes, Hob, Hobble, Hobbles, Hobbies, Hobs, Hose, Hole, Holes, Holies, Hoe, Hoes, Hog, Hogs, His, Hie, Hies.

88 Teacher, Cheater, Hectare.

89 Abdomen, Bureaucrat, Diversion, Flabbergast, Indicate, Longitude, Newspaper, Romantic, Sustenance, Volunteer.

90 T. (The first letter of one, two three etc.)

91 No. The words in the box each begins with one of the vowels in their usual order.

92 Italy, Napoleon, Douglas, Indigo, Apple, Nightmare, Algebra, Jerusalem, Ostrich, Neptune, Emperor, Salami. The character is Indiana Jones.

93 California, Idaho Nebraska, Hawaii, Alaska.

94 Raiders of the Lost Ark.

95 Rain, Snow, Hail, Mist.

96 Spare
Pears
Reaps
Pares
Spear.

97 Rocking Horse.

98 Four, Seven, One, Six. When added together they make eighteen.

99 Sarah, Fiona, George, James.

100 Play time.

101 Earwig, Centipede, Tarantula, Cockroach, Earthworm.

102 See over.

103 Denmark, Canada, Germany, Ireland, New Zealand.

104 Robinson Crusoe
Swiss Family Robinson
The Three Musketeers
Tales of Tom Bombadil
The Chronicles of Narnia.

105 Iceland.

106 She said that that 'that' that I said should have been 'those.'

The culprit made his admission sorrowfully. The day after he was shot.

I said 'and' but he said I said 'but,' but he was wrong and I said so.

ANSWERS

107 Scorned. (All the words contain food.)

108 Noiseless Lionesses.

109
1. Computer.
2. Sinai.
3. Cathedral.
4. Pizza.
5. Goldfish.
6. Ostrich.
7. Magazine.
8. Bicycle.

110 Ursa Major
Orion
Horse Nebula
Neptune
Venus
Betelgeuse
Pluto
Perseids
Halley's Comet.

111
1. All that glitters (glisters) is not gold.
2. A rolling stone gathers no moss.
3. The grass is always greener on the other side of the fence.
4. Set a thief to catch a thief.
5. Troubles always seem to come in threes.

112 Butter
Totter
Barrel
Longer
Rubble
Totals.

113 Hand.

102

114 Accountant, Pilot, Teacher, Nurse, Discjockey.

115 Bedtime story.

116 Herd, Clutch, Gaggle, Pride, School.

117
1. Attention
2. Nitrogen
3. Nugget
4. Tolerable
5. Eerie
6. Eggplant
7. Tortoise
8. Eyewitness
9. Squabble
10. Execution
11. Nothing.

118 Chestnut
Lime
Redwood
Laburnum
Douglas Fir

119 Catapult. (All the words include the name of an animal.)

120 Here we go round the Mulberry Bush.
What big eyes you have Grand mama.
The Lion, the Witch and the Wardrobe.
Little Bo Peep she lost her sheep.

121 A B E H I.

122 Snake, Ache, Bake, Rake, Wake, Forsake, Lake, Break, Stake, Fake.

123 The Hobbit –
J.R.R. Tolkien
James and the Giant Peach
– Roald Dahl,
The House at Pooh Corner
– A.A. Milne
Finn Family Moomintroll
– Tove Jannson
Tom Sawyer – Mark Twain
White Fang – Jack London.

124
1. Rain
2. Sun
3. Snow
4. Hail.

125 Pimento. This is also the name of a food.

126 The correct order is wolf, taxi, hair, ache.
Fire is the thing which is hot.

127 To swim like a fish
To fly like a bird
To rain cats and dogs
To run like the wind
To smell like a rose.

128 Primrose
Buttercup
Daisy
Bluebell
Heather.

129 Rotate
Succulent
Dishwasher
Hostile
Nocturnal
Frontier
Lacerate
Unfurl
Misjudge
Quarterly

130 Saxophone.

131 Modicum
Cadmium
Academic
Dummied
Acceded.

132 Bugs, (all curved letters – no straight lines).

133
1. Harvard
2. Bangkok
3. Buttercup
4. Marsupial
5. Roulette
6. Diamond
7. Deciduous
8. Scotland
9. Cannibal
10. Planet.

134 Farmer
Fields
Horses
Cereal
Fences.

135 Sea of Tranquility.

136 Oblique
Infinity
Arrogance
Convalesce
Millennium
Subliminal
Humanoid
Ingenuity
Rudimentary
Bouquet.

137 Bill and Ted's Excellent
Adventure.
Around the World in
Eighty Days.
The Purple Rose of Cairo.
My Stepmother is an Alien.
The Importance of Being
Earnest.

138 See next page.

139 Loyal,
Spoil
Royal
Toil
Gargoyle.

140 Fridge
Microwave
Kettle
Oven
Saucer.

141 Disaster.

142 Blackguard
Blueberry
Blueprint
Blackbeard
Greenhouse

143 Ate pill.

144 Green Brian
(Big Ben, Old Glory,
Union Jack, Blue Beard
Stormin' Norman).

145 See over. Theme is the
word that appears twice.

146 First
Fist
Sift
Lift
Flit
Fit
Fig.

147 Tom Cruise.

148 Cat, Ant, Rat, Bat, Dog.

149 1. Just in time.
2. Cloud burst.
3. Isabel.
4. Shipwreck.
5. One thing after another.
6. Step by step.
7. Fiddler on the Roof.
8. The last resort.
9. Piggy in the middle.
10. Mixed nuts.
11. Young at Heart.
12. Jumble sale.
13. Rule the roost

150 E. (The second letter of
January, February,
March etc.)

151 The correct order is bird,
book, vase, chef.
The flower is rose.

152 Staple, Pastel, Palest,
Plates, Pleats, Petals.

153 Latin.

154 Bugle, Attack, Tank
Tactics, Lieutenant,
Enemy. The word is battle.

155 Mother Goose.

156 Elation, All, Slope, Pasta,
Red, Ordain, Barrier.
Breeds of Dog: Spaniel,
Poodle, Alsatian, Labrador,
Terrier.

157 1. Hockey.
2. Cycling.
3. Badminton.
4. Riding.
5. Karate.
6. Skating.

158 Ski, Camp, Hail, Ocean, Olden, Lapel.
The answer is school.

159 1. Mansfield Park
– Jane Austen.
2. Hard Times
– Charles Dickens.
3. Romeo and Juliet
– William Shakespeare.
4. Tess of the d'Urbervilles
– Thomas Hardy.

160 Denmark, Iran, Canada, Germany, China.

161 Light
Spark
Shine
Gleam
Flame.

162 Igloo.

163 See over.
Janet Jackson is missing.

164 Electric, Longer, Ember, Cricket, Tablet, Rosemary, Oregano, Dawdle, Eternal.
The word is electrode.

165 A.

166 Teddy bear.

167 Cat, Dog, Fish, Hamster.

168 Laura, Freddy, Sally, Tony.

169 Too many chiefs and not enough Indians.
Many hands make light work.
An apple a day keeps the doctor away.

138

J	H	A	C	D	J	U	L	V	Q
O	S	R	T	S	U	L	N	I	P
A	P	V	D	N	E	S	I	E	A
N	E	W	K	I	P	Q	U	R	H
C	T	E	L	J	C	S	O	G	T
Y	Q	T	E	I	U	K	Z	X	C
R	E	L	L	E	H	C	I	M	R
R	V	A	K	L	T	E	B	O	J
A	T	U	H	O	L	L	Y	Y	S
L	K	L	H	O	P	R	U	T	G

A new broom sweeps clean.
A stitch in time saves nine.
Cut your coat according to
your cloth.
When the cat's away the
mouse will play.
Can't see the wood for the
trees.
All's well that ends well.
It's an ill wind that blows.
nobody any good.

170 32.

171 Large elephants seldom
walk quickly.
Hamsters never take lunch
with crocodiles.
Even small giraffes sleep
standing.
Beautiful butterflies flitter
among flowers.
Giant pandas dwell among
bamboo groves.
All the words have their first
halves after their second.

145

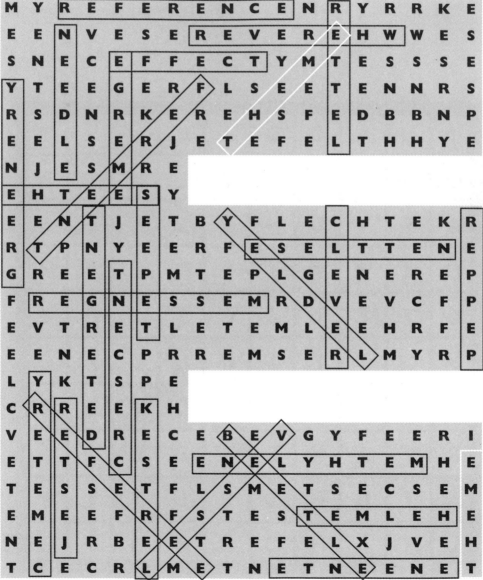